How To Talk About Money?

How To Talk About Money?

Understanding Your Money Mindset 1
Establishing Open Communication about Money 10
Creating a Joint Budget and Expense Plan 19
Resolving Conflicts and Differences in Money Management 29
Working Together to Save and Invest 39
Planning for Big Financial Decisions Together 69
Dealing with Debt and Financial Challenges as a Team 81
Strategies for Sharing Expenses Fairly 90
Strategies for Sharing Expenses Fairly 101
Celebrating Financial Milestones 111
The Power of Financial Freedom 120
Embracing Financial Independence 129
The Impact of Financial Literacy 138
Building Generational Wealth 147
Mastering the Art of Financial Resilience 158

1.
2.
3.
4.
5.
6.
7.
8.
9.
10.
11.
12.
13.
14.

Understanding Your Money Mindset

Exploring Your Relationship with Money

Money plays a crucial role in our lives, influencing not only our financial well-being but also our emotions, relationships, and overall sense of security. Our relationship with money is deeply intertwined with our beliefs, experiences, and values, shaping how we view and interact with wealth.

When we explore our relationship with money, we delve into the complexities of our financial mindset. It involves reflecting on our upbringing, experiences, and societal influences that have contributed to our current perceptions of money. By examining our past financial decisions and behaviors, we gain insight into the patterns and habits that guide our financial choices.

Understanding our relationship with money also requires us to confront our fears, insecurities, and aspirations related to finances. It involves examining the emotional attachments we have to money, whether it be a source of stress, security, or freedom. By acknowledging our emotional responses to money, we can begin to unravel the underlying beliefs and values that drive our financial decisions.

Exploring our relationship with money is a journey of self-discovery and introspection, providing an opportunity to gain clarity on our financial motivations and priorities. By delving into our money mindset, we lay the foundation for transforming our beliefs and behaviors around money, ultimately leading to a healthier and more empowered approach to managing our finances.

Unpacking Your Money Beliefs and Values

Money beliefs and values are deeply ingrained in our minds and guide our financial decisions. They influence how we earn, spend, save, and invest our money. Unpacking these beliefs and values involves reflecting on what money means to us and how it shapes our attitudes and behaviors.

Consider the messages you received about money from your family, culture, and society. Were you taught that money is scarce and hard to come by, or that it flows abundantly and effortlessly? Do you view money as a source of security, freedom, power, or something else entirely?

Reflect on your core values and how they align with your financial choices. Are you driven by a desire for material wealth, personal fulfillment, social responsibility, or a combination of these? Understanding your money beliefs and values can reveal underlying motivations and help you align your financial goals with your deepest desires and aspirations.

Take time to explore any conflicting beliefs or values you may have about money. Do you feel guilty about spending on yourself, or do you have a fear of running out of money? Identify these internal conflicts and consider how they may be impacting your financial decisions and overall well-being.

By unpacking your money beliefs and values, you can gain insights into your financial mindset and begin to make more conscious and intentional choices about money. This self-awareness is a crucial step towards creating a healthy and balanced relationship with money that aligns with your values and aspirations.

Recognizing How Your Upbringing Influenced Your Money Mindset

Our upbringing plays a critical role in shaping our money mindset. The beliefs and values instilled in us during childhood can have a lasting impact on how we view and manage money as adults. Whether we were raised in a household where money was openly discussed and valued, or in an environment where financial struggles were constant, our early experiences greatly influence our financial behaviors and attitudes.

The way our parents or caregivers handled money, the messages they conveyed about wealth and success, and the lessons we learned from observing their financial decisions all contribute to our money mindset. If we grew up in a family that prioritized saving, budgeting, and investing wisely, we may have developed healthy financial habits. Conversely, if money was a source of stress, conflict, or secrecy in our childhood home, we may carry emotional baggage and limiting beliefs about money into adulthood.

Recognizing how our upbringing has influenced our money mindset is the first step towards understanding why we think and act the way we do when it comes to finances. By examining our past experiences and reflecting on the lessons we learned about money while growing up, we can gain insight into the roots of our current financial behaviors and beliefs. This awareness allows us to challenge any negative or limiting beliefs we may have inherited and empowers us to make intentional choices about our relationship with money.

Identifying Your Money Triggers and Emotional Responses

Identifying Your Money Triggers and Emotional Responses

Understanding your money triggers is essential to gaining insight into your financial behaviors and decision-making processes. These triggers are often deeply rooted in your past experiences, beliefs, and emotions surrounding money. By identifying and acknowledging these triggers, you can begin to recognize how they influence your financial actions and mindset.

Take time to reflect on situations or events that provoke strong emotional responses related to money. It could be a fear of scarcity stemming from childhood experiences, feelings of guilt or shame associated with overspending, or anxiety about financial uncertainty. These triggers can manifest in various ways, such as impulsive shopping, hoarding money, or avoiding financial discussions altogether.

Once you have identified your money triggers, consider how they impact your financial decisions. Do you tend to overspend when stressed or seek comfort in retail therapy when feeling down? Are you overly cautious with your money due to a fear of losing financial security? Recognizing these patterns can help you develop strategies to address and manage your emotional responses in more constructive ways.

It's important to remember that everyone has their unique money triggers and emotional reactions. By acknowledging and understanding yours, you can begin to take control of your financial well-being and make more conscious choices aligned with your values and goals. Engaging in open conversations with trusted individuals or seeking professional support can also be beneficial in navigating and overcoming challenging money triggers.

Examining the Impact of Societal Norms on Your Money Mindset

Our societal norms play a significant role in shaping our attitudes towards money and financial success. From a young age, we are exposed to societal messages that dictate what success looks like, often equating it with material wealth and possessions. These messages can create pressure to conform to certain standards of living and spending, leading to feelings of inadequacy or insecurity if we fall short.

The pressure to keep up with the Joneses can be overwhelming, pushing us to spend beyond our means in order to portray a certain image of success. This can lead to financial stress and instability as we try to live up to societal expectations rather than staying true to our own values and priorities.

Furthermore, societal norms can also influence how we view ourselves in relation to others based on our financial status. Comparing ourselves to others can breed feelings of envy, competitiveness, and even shame if we perceive ourselves as less successful or wealthy. This comparison trap can erode our self-worth and distort our perceptions of what truly matters in life.

It is important to recognize the impact of societal norms on our money mindset in order to break free from negative patterns and cultivate a healthier relationship with money. By questioning and challenging these norms, we can begin to redefine success on our own terms, based on our values, goals, and aspirations. This shift towards a more authentic and empowered mindset can lead to greater financial well-being and fulfillment in the long run.

Understanding the Role of Media and Advertising in Shaping Your Financial Thoughts

Media and advertising play a significant role in shaping our financial thoughts and behaviors. From commercials promoting the latest products to social media influencers flaunting luxurious lifestyles, we are constantly bombarded with messages that influence our spending habits and financial decisions. These messages often create a sense of inadequacy or FOMO (fear of missing out), leading us to believe that we need to buy more to be happy or successful.

Advertisers strategically target our emotions and desires, leveraging psychological tactics to convince us that we need their products or services to feel fulfilled. They create a culture of consumerism, where the value of a person is often equated with their material possessions. This can lead to unhealthy financial habits, such as overspending, impulse buying, and accumulating debt to keep up with societal expectations.

It is crucial to be aware of the manipulation tactics used in advertising and media to safeguard our financial well-being. By questioning the messages we are exposed to and being mindful of our reactions, we can resist the pressure to conform to unrealistic standards of wealth and success. Developing a critical eye towards marketing strategies can empower us to make more informed choices and prioritize our financial goals based on our values and needs rather than external influences.

In a world saturated with advertisements and media messages, cultivating a sense of discernment is essential for maintaining financial stability and creating a healthy relationship with money. By recognizing the impact of media and advertising on our financial thoughts, we can take control of our financial narrative and make decisions that align with our long-term financial well-being.

Reflecting on Past Financial Experiences and Lessons Learned

Reflecting on Past Financial Experiences and Lessons Learned

As you look back on your financial journey, take a moment to consider the highs and lows, the wins and losses that have shaped your current financial mindset. Reflect on the decisions you've made, the risks you've taken, and the outcomes that have ensued. What were the pivotal moments that taught you valuable lessons about money? How have past experiences influenced your current attitudes and behaviors towards finances?

Think about the times when you felt a sense of accomplishment and financial stability. What were the factors that contributed to those moments of success? On the flip side, recall the times when you faced financial challenges or setbacks. What were the mistakes or missteps that led to those difficult situations? What did you learn from those experiences that you can apply to your financial decisions moving forward?

Consider the role of financial education and awareness in shaping your past experiences. Have there been instances where lack of knowledge or understanding about financial concepts has impacted your choices? How have you sought to improve your financial literacy over time? Reflect on the resources and tools that have helped you navigate complex financial situations and make informed decisions.

Take a moment to think about the relationship between your past financial experiences and your current financial goals. How have past successes and failures influenced the goals you have set for yourself? Are there patterns or tendencies in your financial behavior that stem from past experiences? What adjustments or changes can you make based on the lessons you've learned along the way?

Remember that reflecting on past financial experiences is not about dwelling on mistakes or missed opportunities. Instead, it is about gaining insight and wisdom from your journey so far. By acknowledging the lessons learned and applying them to your future financial endeavors, you can move forward with greater confidence and clarity in managing your money.

Assessing Your Risk Tolerance and Attitude Towards Money

Assessing your risk tolerance and attitude towards money requires a deep introspection into your financial mindset. Do you tend to play it safe, avoiding any risks that could potentially lead to financial loss? Or are you more inclined to take calculated risks in pursuit of greater rewards? Understanding your risk tolerance is crucial in making informed financial decisions. It involves evaluating how comfortable you are with uncertainty, fluctuations in the market, and the possibility of loss. Your attitude towards money plays a significant role in shaping your risk tolerance. Are you a conservative saver who prioritizes security and stability, or are you a more adventurous investor willing to take chances for potentially higher returns? Reflecting on your past financial experiences and observing how you responded to different situations can provide valuable insights into your risk tolerance and attitude towards money. Consider how you felt during times of financial uncertainty or when faced with investment opportunities. Did you feel anxious, excited, or confident? These emotional responses can indicate your comfort level with risk and volatility. It is essential to strike a balance between risk and reward that aligns with your financial goals and values. By assessing your risk tolerance and attitude towards money, you can make more informed decisions that serve your long-term financial well-being.

Embracing Self-Awareness and Growth in Your Money Mindset

Self-awareness is the foundation upon which true growth and transformation in your money mindset can occur. It requires a deep introspection into your thoughts, beliefs, and behaviors surrounding money. As you embark on this journey of self-discovery, be prepared to confront your fears, biases, and limitations with honesty and courage. Take the time to reflect on your past financial decisions and the underlying motivations behind them. Consider how your upbringing, cultural background, and social environment have shaped your attitudes towards money. By acknowledging your financial strengths and weaknesses, you can gain valuable insights into areas where you need to grow and evolve. Embrace the discomfort that may arise from challenging your existing beliefs and be open to new perspectives and possibilities. Remember that self-awareness is not a destination but a continuous process of learning and unlearning. Through this process, you can cultivate a healthier and more empowering relationship with money that aligns with your values and goals.

Setting Goals for Changing and Improving Your Relationship with Money

To begin changing and improving your relationship with money, it's crucial to set clear and achievable goals. These goals serve as a roadmap towards financial growth and stability while also providing motivation and direction in your money mindset journey. Start by assessing your current financial situation and identifying areas that need improvement. Whether it's increasing your savings rate, paying off debt, investing more, or earning additional income, outlining specific objectives will help you stay focused and track your progress.

When setting financial goals, it's important to make them SMART: Specific, Measurable, Achievable, Relevant, and Time-bound. Specific goals are clear and detailed, making it easier to know exactly what you're working towards. Measurable goals allow you to track your progress and celebrate small victories along the way. Ensure that your goals are achievable based on your current circumstances and resources. Make them relevant to your overall financial objectives and values. Lastly, set a timeline for each goal to create a sense of urgency and accountability.

Consider both short-term and long-term goals to balance immediate needs with future aspirations. Short-term goals could include building an emergency fund, eliminating high-interest debt, or starting a retirement savings account. Long-term goals may involve purchasing a home, funding your children's education, or achieving financial independence. By establishing a mix of goals that align with your values and priorities, you can create a well-rounded financial plan that addresses various aspects of your financial well-being.

Moreover, don't be afraid to dream big when setting your financial goals. While it's important to be realistic, pushing yourself outside your comfort zone can lead to significant growth and accomplishments. Visualize your ideal financial future and set ambitious but attainable goals that inspire and motivate you to take action. Remember that progress may not always be linear, and setbacks are a natural part of any journey towards financial empowerment. Stay resilient, adaptable, and committed to your goals, adjusting them as needed to reflect changes in your life circumstances and priorities. By setting clear and meaningful financial goals, you can transform your money mindset and pave the way for a more secure and prosperous financial future.

Establishing Open Communication about Money

Importance of Transparent Communication

Open, honest, and transparent communication about money is the cornerstone of a healthy financial relationship. It lays the foundation for understanding each other's perspectives, values, and goals when it comes to finances. Transparency eliminates misunderstandings and fosters trust, creating a safe space for discussing even the most sensitive financial matters. By sharing openly about your financial situation, concerns, and aspirations, you can work together towards a common vision for your future. It allows you to make informed decisions that align with both your individual and collective objectives. Without transparency, misunderstandings and conflicts can arise, leading to resentment, miscommunication, and ultimately jeopardizing the stability of your financial partnership. Therefore, prioritizing transparent communication ensures that both partners feel heard, valued, and respected in the journey towards financial well-being.

Recognizing Personal Money Mindsets

Understanding our personal money mindsets is crucial for navigating financial discussions with our partners. These mindsets are shaped by our upbringing, experiences, and beliefs about money. Some of us may view money as a source of security, while others may see it as a tool for enjoyment or power. Recognizing these underlying beliefs can help us better understand our own relationship with money and how it influences our financial decisions. By acknowledging and discussing our personal money mindsets, we can work towards aligning our goals and values with those of our partner, paving the way for more productive and harmonious money talks.

Setting Ground Rules for Money Talks

Establishing ground rules for money talks is essential for maintaining productive and respectful discussions about finances within a relationship. These rules create a framework that promotes understanding, transparency, and effective communication. By setting clear guidelines for how money talks should be conducted, couples can navigate financial conversations more smoothly and potentially avoid misunderstandings or conflicts.

1. Establish a Safe Environment: Ensure that discussions about money take place in a calm and private setting where both partners feel comfortable sharing their thoughts and concerns without fear of judgment.

2. Listen with Empathy: Practice active listening during money talks, truly hearing and understanding your partner's perspective without interrupting or dismissing their feelings. Show empathy and respect for their viewpoint.

3. Use "I" Statements: When expressing your own thoughts or concerns about finances, use "I" statements to take ownership of your feelings and avoid sounding accusatory. For example, say "I feel stressed about our budget" instead of "You always overspend."

4. Set a Time Limit: Agree on a reasonable time frame for money discussions to prevent them from dragging on or becoming overwhelming. This can help keep the conversation focused and productive.

5. Stay Focused on the Issue at Hand: Avoid bringing up past grievances or unrelated topics during money talks. Stay focused on the specific financial matter being discussed to make progress towards a resolution.

6. Be Open to Compromise: Understand that financial decisions often require compromise. Approach money talks with a willingness to find common ground and work together towards mutually beneficial solutions.

7. Seek Professional Help if Needed: If money talks become too challenging or if couples struggle to find common ground, consider seeking the help of a financial advisor, counselor, or therapist to facilitate conversations and offer guidance.

8. Agree on Actions Steps: Conclude money talks with clear action steps and responsibilities for each partner to address the financial issue at hand. Setting concrete plans can help avoid misunderstandings and ensure progress is made.

By establishing these ground rules for money talks, couples can create a structured and positive environment for discussing finances, leading to stronger communication and a healthier financial relationship.

Creating a Safe Space for Financial Discussions

Establishing a safe space for financial discussions is crucial in fostering open communication and trust between partners. Creating an environment where both individuals feel respected, heard, and understood can lead to more productive and healthy conversations about money matters. Here are some key strategies to help you create a safe space for discussing finances:

Set aside dedicated time for money talks without distractions. Agree to listen actively and without judgment. Be honest and transparent about your financial situation and feelings. Respect each other's perspectives, even if you disagree. Focus on finding solutions and compromising when needed. Practice empathy and understanding towards each other's money histories and experiences. Refrain from blaming or criticizing each other; instead, work together as a team. Keep discussions confidential and avoid sharing personal financial details with others. Remain calm and composed, even during difficult conversations. Remember that discussing finances is a collaborative effort aimed at strengthening your relationship and financial future. By creating a safe space for financial discussions, you can build a solid foundation of trust and communication that will benefit your partnership in the long run.

Addressing Past Money Baggage

Addressing Past Money Baggage

Unpacking past experiences with money can be a crucial step in establishing a healthy financial foundation with your partner. Many of us carry emotional baggage related to money from our upbringing or past relationships. This baggage can manifest as fears, insecurities, or triggers that impact our current financial decisions.

It's essential to take the time to reflect on your own money history and understand how it has shaped your attitudes and behaviors towards money. Be honest with yourself about any negative beliefs or patterns that you may be carrying from the past. Recognizing these patterns is the first step towards breaking free from them.

When discussing past money baggage with your partner, approach the conversation with empathy and understanding. Share your own experiences openly and encourage your partner to do the same. Listen attentively and validate each other's feelings without judgment.

Work together to identify any recurring money themes or conflicts that may stem from your past. By shining a light on these issues, you can begin to address them as a team and find healthier ways to approach financial matters in your relationship.

Remember, addressing past money baggage is not about assigning blame or dwelling on the past. It's about acknowledging the impact that previous experiences have had on your financial mindset and working together to create a new narrative for your shared financial future. By confronting these challenges head-on, you can pave the way for a more harmonious and fulfilling financial journey with your partner.

Sharing Financial Goals and Values

When it comes to sharing financial goals and values, it is essential for couples to have open and honest discussions about their aspirations and beliefs surrounding money. This aspect of a relationship can often reveal deep-seated values and expectations that may have developed over time. By sharing these aspects of your financial mindset, you are not only aligning your goals but also gaining a deeper understanding of each other's perspectives.

This exchange of information can lead to a more cohesive approach to managing finances as a couple. It allows you to identify common goals that you can work towards together, whether it be saving for a home, starting a family, or investing in your future. By understanding each other's values when it comes to money, you can create a financial plan that reflects your shared vision and aspirations.

Moreover, discussing financial goals and values can help you prioritize what is truly important to both of you. By having these conversations, you can ensure that your financial decisions are aligned with your core values and aspirations. This can lead to a sense of unity and purpose in your financial journey as a couple.

Overall, sharing your financial goals and values is a crucial step in building a strong foundation for your joint financial future. It allows you to understand each other's perspectives, align your aspirations, and create a roadmap for achieving your shared goals. By openly discussing your financial values, you can strengthen your relationship, enhance your communication, and work together towards a secure and prosperous future.

Handling Financial Responsibilities and Contributions

Handling Financial Responsibilities and Contributions

It is essential for couples to establish clear guidelines for handling financial responsibilities and contributions within their relationship. This includes determining how expenses will be divided, who will be responsible for certain financial tasks, and how each partner's income will be utilized to meet shared goals.

Open and honest communication is key when discussing financial responsibilities. Both partners should feel comfortable expressing their expectations, concerns, and preferences regarding money matters. By discussing and agreeing on financial responsibilities early on, couples can prevent misunderstandings and potential conflicts down the road.

When determining how expenses will be divided, partners should consider their respective incomes, financial goals, and spending habits. Some couples may choose to split expenses evenly, while others may opt for a proportional arrangement based on income levels. It is important to find a system that feels fair and equitable to both parties.

In addition to day-to-day expenses, couples should also discuss how they will handle larger financial responsibilities such as major purchases, investments, and saving for the future. Establishing a plan for how these decisions will be made can help prevent disagreements and ensure that both partners have a say in important financial matters.

Contributions to joint accounts, savings goals, and retirement accounts should also be discussed and agreed upon. Each partner should feel comfortable with their level of contribution and understand how their money is being used to support their shared financial future. Regular check-ins to review and adjust contributions can help ensure that both partners remain on track towards their financial goals.

By openly discussing and agreeing on financial responsibilities and contributions, couples can build a strong foundation for financial harmony and stability in their relationship.

Developing a System for Regular Money Check-Ins

Regular money check-ins are a crucial part of maintaining financial harmony in a relationship. These check-ins serve as a way to track progress towards financial goals, address any emerging issues, and ensure that both partners are on the same page when it comes to money matters. Setting up a system for regular money discussions can help prevent misunderstandings, build trust, and strengthen your financial partnership over time.

To begin, establish a schedule for your money check-ins that works for both partners. This could be a weekly, bi-weekly, or monthly meeting dedicated to discussing your finances. Consistency is key to making these discussions a habit and ensuring that important financial matters are consistently addressed.

During your money check-ins, review your budget, expenses, and savings progress together. Take the time to discuss any changes in income, upcoming expenses, or financial goals that may need to be adjusted. This is also an opportunity to celebrate milestones, such as reaching a savings goal or paying off a debt.

Consider using this time to address any financial concerns or questions that may have arisen since your last check-in. Encourage open communication and be prepared to listen actively to your partner's thoughts and ideas. Remember, the goal of these discussions is to work together towards a shared financial future.

Keep track of your financial discussions and decisions by documenting key points and action items from each check-in. This can help you stay accountable and track your progress over time. Additionally, consider setting short-term and long-term financial goals together to guide your money conversations and ensure you are both working towards a common objective.

Remember, regular money check-ins are not just about numbers and spreadsheets; they are about building a strong foundation of communication and trust in your relationship. By making these discussions a priority and approaching them with a proactive mindset, you can navigate your financial journey together with confidence and unity.

Dealing with Conflicts and Disagreements Constructively

Conflicts and disagreements about money can arise in any relationship, and it is essential to address them constructively to maintain a healthy financial partnership. When faced with financial disagreements, it is crucial to approach the situation with empathy and open-mindedness. Listen actively to your partner's perspective and try to understand their underlying concerns and motivations. Avoid assigning blame or becoming defensive, as this can escalate tensions and hinder productive communication.

Instead, focus on finding common ground and working together towards a mutually beneficial solution. Set aside dedicated time to discuss the issue calmly and rationally, allowing both parties to share their viewpoints without interruption. Practice active listening and strive to empathize with your partner's financial needs and goals.

When navigating financial conflicts, remember that compromise is key. Be willing to meet halfway and explore alternative solutions that address both partners' concerns. Keep the lines of communication open and be willing to revisit the discussion as needed to ensure that both partners feel heard and respected. Through respectful communication and a willingness to collaborate, you can overcome financial conflicts and strengthen your relationship in the process.

Cultivating Trust and Mutual Understanding in Money Matters

Trust is the foundation of a strong financial partnership. Without trust, misunderstandings and conflicts can easily arise, leading to strain in the relationship. Building trust in money matters requires transparency, honesty, and mutual respect. It is essential to have open and honest conversations about finances, share financial responsibilities, and work together towards common goals. Trust is not built overnight but is developed through consistent communication, respecting each other's views, and being accountable for your actions. By cultivating trust in money matters, you create a solid groundwork for a healthy financial partnership built on mutual understanding and respect.

Creating a Joint Budget and Expense Plan

Setting Financial Goals Together

Setting financial goals together is a crucial step towards building a solid foundation for your future as a couple. It requires open communication, alignment, and a shared vision of what you want to achieve financially. By discussing both short-term and long-term goals, you can create a roadmap that will guide your financial decisions and actions. Setting specific, measurable, achievable, relevant, and time-bound (SMART) goals can help you stay focused and motivated on your journey towards financial success. Take the time to understand each other's priorities, dreams, and values when it comes to money. This will help you identify common goals that reflect your shared values and aspirations. Whether it's saving for a down payment on a home, planning for retirement, or traveling the world together, setting financial goals as a couple can strengthen your bond and bring you closer as partners. Remember, your financial goals are not set in stone and can evolve over time. Regularly reviewing and revising your goals will ensure that they remain aligned with your current circumstances and aspirations. By working together to set clear and achievable financial goals, you can pave the way for a more secure and fulfilling future for both of you.

Assessing Current Financial Situation

Assessing Current Financial Situation

Understanding your current financial situation is crucial in building a strong foundation for your financial goals as a couple. Begin by gathering information about your income sources, expenses, debts, and savings. Take an honest look at your financial health and identify areas where improvements can be made.

Review your monthly income streams, including salaries, bonuses, investments, and any other sources of revenue. Calculate your total household income and consider any fluctuations or irregularities in earnings.

Next, examine your monthly expenses in detail. Track all your spending habits, from fixed expenses like rent or mortgage payments to variable costs such as groceries, utilities, and entertainment. Identify areas where you may be overspending or where there is room for adjustment.

Now, turn your attention to your existing debts, such as credit card balances, loans, or outstanding payments. Determine the total amount of debt owed and the corresponding interest rates. Create a plan to pay off debt systematically, starting with high-interest debts to save money in the long run.

Evaluate your current savings and investments. Determine how much you have saved in emergency funds, retirement accounts, or other investment vehicles. Assess the performance of your investments and consider diversifying your portfolio for long-term financial growth.

By assessing your current financial situation together, you gain a clear understanding of where you stand financially as a couple. This knowledge will inform your decision-making process as you move forward in establishing a shared budget framework and working towards your financial goals.

Establishing a Shared Budget Framework

To establish a shared budget framework, it is crucial for couples to come together and have open discussions about their financial priorities and objectives. This process involves aligning individual values and goals to create a unified vision for their financial future.

By setting clear intentions and being transparent about financial aspirations, couples can create a strong foundation for their budget planning.

One key aspect of establishing a shared budget framework is agreeing on budget categories and allocations based on mutual priorities. This involves identifying essential expenses, such as housing, utilities, and groceries, as well as discretionary spending, such as entertainment and dining out. By outlining these categories and determining how much to allocate to each, couples can ensure that their budget reflects their shared values and financial objectives.

Creating a realistic budget that accounts for both partners' needs and wants is essential for long-term financial success. This requires compromise and understanding, as each partner may have different spending habits or financial priorities. By openly discussing and negotiating budget allocations, couples can find a balance that allows them to meet their needs while also working towards their shared financial goals.

In addition to setting budget categories and allocations, it is important for couples to establish a system for tracking expenses and monitoring progress. This can involve using budgeting apps, spreadsheets, or other tools to keep track of spending and ensure that they are staying within their budget. By regularly reviewing their budget performance and making adjustments as needed, couples can stay on track towards achieving their financial objectives and maintaining financial stability.

Overall, establishing a shared budget framework is a collaborative process that requires communication, compromise, and mutual understanding. By working together to create a budget that reflects their shared goals and values, couples can build a solid financial foundation and set themselves up for long-term financial success.

Tracking Expenses and Monitoring Progress

Tracking Expenses and Monitoring Progress

To effectively manage your joint finances, it is crucial to track your expenses and monitor your progress towards your financial goals. Tracking expenses allows you to understand where your money is going and identify areas where you can make adjustments to stay within your budget. By monitoring your progress regularly, you can stay on track and make informed decisions about your financial future. Here are some key strategies for tracking expenses and monitoring progress as a couple:

1. Keep Detailed Records: Make it a habit to record all expenses, whether big or small. Use a budgeting tool or app to categorize expenses and track spending across different categories.

2. Review Regularly: Set aside time each week or month to review your expenses and compare them to your budget. This regular check-in helps you stay aware of your financial habits and identify any deviations from your plan.

3. Identify Patterns: Look for patterns in your spending behavior. Are there recurring expenses that can be reduced or eliminated? Identifying these patterns can help you make more informed decisions about your budget.

4. Set Milestones: Establish milestones or checkpoints to measure your progress towards your financial goals. Celebrate achievements and adjust your strategies if needed to stay on course.

5. Communicate Openly: Share insights from your tracking efforts with your partner. Discuss any concerns or successes in managing expenses and work together to address any challenges that arise.

6. Stay Accountable: Hold each other accountable for sticking to the budget and tracking expenses accurately. Regular communication and transparency are key to successfully managing your joint finances.

7. Adjust as Needed: Be prepared to adjust your budget and expense plan based on your tracking results. If certain expenses are consistently exceeding your budget, discuss ways to reallocate funds or reduce costs in other areas.

By tracking your expenses and monitoring your progress together, you can build a strong financial foundation as a couple and work towards achieving your shared financial goals. It requires commitment, communication, and collaboration, but the rewards of financial stability and security are well worth the effort.

Making Financial Decisions Together

Financial decisions are the cornerstone of a successful partnership. When it comes to managing money as a couple, it is essential to approach decision-making as a team. Each decision, whether big or small, has the potential to impact your financial future. By making financial decisions together, you can ensure that you are both on the same page and working towards shared goals.

Effective communication is key when it comes to making financial decisions as a couple. It is crucial to openly discuss and consider each other's perspectives before reaching a conclusion. By listening to each other's ideas and concerns, you can make more informed decisions that take both partners' needs into account.

When faced with a major financial decision, it is important to weigh the pros and cons together. Consider how the decision aligns with your shared financial goals and budget. Evaluate the potential risks and rewards, and make a decision that you both feel comfortable with.

Remember that financial decisions are not just about the numbers; they also reflect your values and priorities as a couple. By making decisions that reflect your shared values, you can strengthen your bond and build a solid foundation for your financial future.

In the end, working together to make financial decisions can lead to a stronger, more cohesive relationship. By approaching money management as a team, you can navigate challenges and celebrate achievements together. Remember, the power of two is always greater than the sum of its parts when it comes to managing your finances as a couple.

Managing Individual and Joint Accounts

Managing Individual and Joint Accounts

When it comes to managing individual and joint accounts as a couple, it is essential to approach this aspect of your finances with open communication, transparency, and a shared understanding of your financial goals. Each partner brings their own financial history, habits, and responsibilities to the table, which can impact how you choose to handle your accounts.

Combining finances in a relationship can be a significant step towards building a shared future, but it's crucial to determine the most suitable approach for managing your money together. Some couples may opt for fully joint accounts, where all income and expenses are shared, while others may prefer to maintain separate accounts for personal spending while also having a joint account for household expenses.

Regardless of the setup you choose, it's important to establish clear guidelines for how individual and joint accounts will be managed. This could include determining how bills will be paid, how contributions to joint expenses will be made, and how discretionary spending will be handled.

Maintaining transparency in financial transactions is key to building trust and ensuring that both partners are on the same page when it comes to money matters. Regularly reviewing account statements together, discussing any discrepancies or concerns, and making decisions jointly on financial priorities can help strengthen your financial partnership.

Additionally, setting aside time to discuss your financial goals, track your progress, and make adjustments as needed can help you stay aligned and focused on your shared objectives. By working together to manage individual and joint accounts effectively, you can strengthen your financial foundation and set yourselves up for long-term financial success as a couple.

Planning for Emergencies and Contingencies

Emergencies and unexpected events can arise at any moment, impacting our finances and causing stress. It is essential for couples to proactively plan for such contingencies to ensure financial stability and peace of mind. Building an emergency fund is a crucial step in preparing for unforeseen circumstances. By setting aside a designated amount of money each month, couples can create a safety net to cover expenses in the event of job loss, medical emergencies, or unexpected home repairs.

In addition to establishing an emergency fund, it is important for couples to review their insurance coverage to ensure adequate protection against potential financial risks. This includes health insurance, life insurance, disability insurance, and property insurance. Understanding the terms and coverage of each policy is essential in preparing for potential emergencies that may require financial resources beyond what the emergency fund can cover.

Creating a contingency plan for various scenarios, such as loss of income or major expenses, can provide couples with a sense of security and preparedness. By discussing and developing a plan together, couples can identify potential risks and outline steps to mitigate their impact on their finances. This may involve revisiting the budget to reallocate funds for emergency situations or exploring alternative income sources in case of job loss.

Being proactive in planning for emergencies and contingencies not only protects couples from financial setbacks but also strengthens their bond as partners. By facing uncertainties together and taking proactive steps to secure their financial future, couples can navigate challenging times with resilience and confidence.

Saving and Investing as a Team

Saving and investing as a team requires a shared commitment to achieving financial goals. By pooling your resources and working together towards a common vision, you can maximize your potential for long-term financial growth and security.

Start by setting clear savings goals that align with your shared objectives. Identify areas where you can cut back on expenses to redirect funds towards your savings accounts. By maintaining open communication and accountability, you can track your progress and make adjustments as needed.

Consider different investment options that align with your risk tolerance and time horizon. Diversifying your investment portfolio can help spread risk and maximize returns over the long term. Work together to research and select investments that align with your financial goals and values.

Regularly review your savings and investment strategies as a team. Monitor market trends and economic conditions to ensure your investments are performing as expected. Stay informed and seek professional advice when needed to make informed decisions about your financial future.

By saving and investing as a team, you can leverage each other's strengths and support each other through challenges. Building a strong financial foundation together will not only help you achieve your short-term goals but also pave the way for long-term financial success and stability.

Communicating Openly About Financial Challenges

Discussing financial challenges openly and honestly is essential for maintaining a healthy financial partnership. It is crucial to create a safe space where both partners can share their concerns and fears without judgment. Avoiding financial discussions or hiding issues can lead to misunderstandings and tension in the relationship. By openly communicating about financial challenges, couples can work together to find solutions and support each other through difficult times. It's important to listen actively to each other's perspectives and feelings, validating emotions and brainstorming potential solutions. Setting aside dedicated time to have these conversations can help prevent conflicts and ensure that both partners are on the same page when facing financial challenges. Remember that overcoming obstacles together can strengthen the bond between partners and lead to a more resilient and united financial future.

Celebrating Financial Milestones Together

As a couple dedicated to financial growth and stability, it is important to cherish and acknowledge the milestones you achieve together on your financial journey. Celebrating these accomplishments not only reinforces your teamwork but also boosts motivation to continue working towards your shared goals. Whether it's reaching a savings target, paying off a significant debt, or achieving a milestone in your investment portfolio, take the time to acknowledge your progress and celebrate your successes.

Marking these financial milestones can be done in various ways that suit your preferences as a couple. Consider having a special dinner at home or dining out at a favorite restaurant to commemorate the achievement. You could also plan a weekend getaway or treat yourselves to a small luxury item that you've been eyeing as a reward for your hard work and dedication to your financial goals.

Another meaningful way to celebrate financial milestones is to reflect on the journey that led you to this point. Take a moment to appreciate the effort, sacrifices, and compromises you both have made along the way. Recognize the strength of your partnership and the trust you have built through open communication and mutual support in managing your finances.

Moreover, sharing your success with loved ones can also be a rewarding experience. Whether it's informing family and friends about your accomplishment or expressing gratitude for their support and encouragement, involving others in your celebration can deepen the sense of achievement and strengthen your relationships.

By celebrating financial milestones together, you not only acknowledge your progress but also reinforce your commitment to your financial goals as a couple. These moments of recognition and appreciation can inspire you to set new targets, overcome challenges, and continue working towards a more secure and prosperous future side by side.

Resolving Conflicts and Differences in Money Management

Understanding Root Causes:

Exploring individual beliefs and experiences with money can often uncover deep-rooted issues that contribute to conflicts in money management. Our upbringing, cultural background, and past financial experiences shape our attitudes and behaviors towards money. By delving into these personal narratives, we can gain insight into the triggers and emotional responses that arise during financial discussions.

Some individuals may have a scarcity mindset due to past financial struggles or a fear of not having enough. Others may have a mindset of abundance, believing that money should be spent freely and without restraint. These contrasting mindsets can lead to clashes when it comes to budgeting, saving, or investing. Understanding these underlying beliefs can help us empathize with our partner's perspective and work towards finding common ground.

Identifying the emotional components tied to financial disagreements is crucial in resolving conflicts. Money is often intertwined with feelings of security, power, and self-worth. Arguments about money may actually be manifestations of deeper issues related to trust, control, or insecurities. By recognizing the emotional layers underlying financial conflicts, we can address the root causes with compassion and sensitivity.

Through open and honest discussions about our individual money mindsets and past experiences, we can create a foundation of understanding and empathy. By acknowledging and exploring these root causes, we pave the way for constructive communication and effective conflict resolution in our journey towards financial unity.

Establishing Communication Guidelines:

Establishing Communication Guidelines:

Communication is the foundation of any successful relationship, especially when it comes to discussing sensitive topics such as money. To ensure productive conversations about finances, it is essential to establish clear and effective communication guidelines as a couple.

Begin by creating a safe and judgment-free space where both partners feel comfortable expressing their thoughts and concerns about money. Practice active listening, which involves giving your full attention to your partner without interrupting or passing judgment. Validate their feelings and perspectives, even if they differ from your own.

Set ground rules for discussing financial matters. Agree on a time and place for these conversations, ensuring that both partners are in a calm and focused state of mind. Avoid bringing up money issues in the heat of the moment or during times of stress.

Implement empathy in your communication approach. Try to understand your partner's point of view and acknowledge their feelings, even if you do not agree with them. Use "I" statements to express your thoughts and emotions without blaming or accusing your partner.

Practice open and honest communication about money. Share your financial goals, fears, and values with each other. Be transparent about your individual financial situations, including income, expenses, debts, and savings. This level of openness fosters trust and understanding in your relationship.

Develop a system for decision-making regarding finances. Establish how major financial decisions will be made, such as budgeting, investments, and large purchases. Consider creating joint financial goals and a plan for achieving them together.

Lastly, remember that communication is a two-way street. Encourage your partner to express their feelings and ideas about money openly, and be willing to listen and compromise when needed. By establishing effective communication guidelines, you can navigate financial discussions with respect, understanding, and unity as a couple.

Addressing Misaligned Priorities:

Discussing and prioritizing financial goals as a couple is a crucial step in addressing misaligned priorities. It's essential to have open and honest conversations about each person's individual goals and values when it comes to money. Take the time to listen to your partner's perspective and share your own aspirations. Understanding where your priorities differ can help you find common ground and make decisions that align with both of your visions for the future. Compromise is key in finding solutions that honor each other's priorities while working towards shared financial goals. Through respectful communication and a willingness to understand each other's perspectives, you can navigate misaligned priorities and create a financial plan that reflects your mutual values and aspirations.

Seeking Professional Guidance:

Seeking professional guidance can be instrumental in navigating financial conflicts and challenges within a relationship. Financial advisors and counselors possess the expertise and impartiality needed to provide valuable insights and solutions tailored to your specific circumstances. Their guidance can help you gain clarity on financial matters, bridge gaps in understanding, and facilitate productive discussions about money.

An experienced financial advisor can offer objective perspectives on managing finances, setting priorities, and aligning goals as a couple. By leveraging their professional knowledge and resources, you can develop a cohesive financial plan that considers both individual aspirations and shared objectives. Additionally, working with a counselor specializing in financial therapy can help address underlying emotional issues that may contribute to conflicts surrounding money.

Professional guidance extends beyond mere financial advice; it encompasses emotional support, conflict resolution techniques, and strategies for enhancing communication within your relationship. These professionals can facilitate conversations, mediate disagreements, and offer strategies for overcoming financial differences constructively.

Furthermore, seeking professional guidance demonstrates a commitment to growth, improvement, and shared financial success as a couple. It signifies a willingness to invest in the health and longevity of your relationship, recognizing that outside expertise can complement your efforts to foster financial harmony and unity. By enlisting the help of professionals, you can gain valuable tools, insights, and strategies to overcome obstacles and build a solid foundation for your financial future together.

Implementing Conflict Resolution Strategies:

When conflicts arise in money management, it is essential to approach the situation with a mindset focused on resolution and understanding. Here are some key strategies to help you navigate and overcome financial disagreements as a couple:

1. Practice Active Listening: Take the time to listen attentively to your partner's perspective without interrupting or formulating a

response. Show empathy and validate their feelings to foster open communication.

2. Communicate Effectively: Clearly express your thoughts and concerns while maintaining a respectful tone. Avoid placing blame and instead focus on finding solutions together.

3. Seek Common Ground: Identify shared goals and values to establish a foundation for resolving conflicts. Emphasize areas of agreement to build upon and work towards mutual objectives.

4. Collaborate on Solutions: Brainstorm together to generate ideas and strategies that address the root of the conflict. Approach the issue as a team, emphasizing cooperation and compromise.

5. Set Boundaries: Clearly define roles and responsibilities in financial decision-making to prevent misunderstandings and conflicts. Establishing boundaries can help create structure and accountability within your partnership.

6. Take a Time-Out if Needed: If emotions are running high during a disagreement, consider taking a break to cool off and reflect before revisiting the conversation. This can prevent arguments from escalating and provide space for clarity.

7. Practice Patience and Understanding: Recognize that resolving conflicts takes time and effort. Be patient with yourself and your partner as you navigate challenging financial discussions.

8. Focus on the Bigger Picture: Keep your shared goals and vision in mind as you work through conflicts. Remember that overcoming disagreements can strengthen your relationship and financial partnership in the long run.

Setting Boundaries and Responsibilities:

Defining roles in money management within a relationship is crucial for establishing clarity and accountability. By setting boundaries and responsibilities, couples can effectively navigate financial decisions and prevent misunderstandings. Each partner should have a clear understanding of their obligations and contributions to the shared financial goals. Communicating openly about expectations and limitations can help create a harmonious balance in managing finances. Establishing these boundaries not only fosters trust and respect but also promotes a sense of partnership and teamwork in handling money matters. When each partner takes ownership of their responsibilities, it cultivates a cooperative environment where mutual support and collaboration thrive. By delineating roles and setting boundaries effectively, couples can work together towards a secure financial future while nurturing a strong and resilient relationship.

Developing a Shared Vision:

Crafting a shared vision for your financial future is essential in fostering unity and alignment within your relationship. It serves as a guiding light that illuminates the path you both wish to walk together, hand in hand, towards your mutual goals. By developing a shared vision, you are not only harmonizing your aspirations but also reinforcing your commitment to each other and your financial journey.

Begin this process by engaging in open and honest discussions about your individual values, dreams, and priorities. Take the time to listen intently to your partner's perspective, understanding their aspirations and fears. Through this dialogue, you can uncover common ground and discover areas where your goals intersect and overlap.

As you delve deeper into the shared vision-building process, reflect on the values that underpin your financial decisions. Consider what legacy you wish to leave behind and what impact you hope to have on future generations. Embrace the opportunity to dream big and envision a future where your financial resources are aligned with your deepest-held values and beliefs.

To solidify your shared vision, put pen to paper and craft a vision statement that encapsulates your collective aspirations. This statement should serve as a guiding principle, a beacon that illuminates the path ahead and reminds you of your shared goals during challenging times. Display this statement prominently in your living space, allowing it to serve as a constant reminder of your joint commitments.

Embrace the process of developing a shared vision with enthusiasm and sincerity, recognizing that this exercise is not just about money but about building a future filled with purpose and meaning. As you embark on this journey together, let your shared vision serve as a source of inspiration, motivation, and connection, guiding you towards a future filled with abundance and fulfillment.

Managing Stress and Emotions:

Managing Stress and Emotions:

Coping with financial stress can be a significant challenge for couples navigating money management together. When disagreements arise or unexpected financial hurdles present themselves, emotions can run high and strain the relationship. It is essential to recognize the impact of stress on both your mental and emotional well-being, as well as the overall dynamic of your partnership.

Communicating openly and honestly about your feelings regarding financial matters is crucial. Allow space for each other to express concerns, fears, and anxieties without judgment. Listen actively and empathetically, seeking to understand the underlying emotions that may be fueling the stress.

Practice self-awareness by acknowledging your individual triggers and stress responses when it comes to money. By understanding how you personally react to financial challenges, you can better manage your emotions and communicate effectively with your partner.

In times of heightened stress, it is essential to prioritize self-care. Take proactive steps to manage stress levels, whether through exercise, meditation, spending time outdoors, or engaging in activities that bring you joy and relaxation. Remember that your mental well-being is intrinsically connected to your financial health.

Seek support from each other and consider reaching out to a professional counselor or therapist if the stress becomes overwhelming. A neutral third party can provide valuable insight and tools to navigate emotional challenges related to money management.

Remember that managing stress and emotions is a continual process. By cultivating healthy coping mechanisms, fostering open communication, and prioritizing self-care, you can strengthen your relationship and navigate financial difficulties more effectively. Together, you can weather the storms and emerge stronger, with a deeper understanding of each other and a shared commitment to your financial well-being.

Moving Forward Constructively:

Reflecting on past conflicts can provide valuable insights into areas for improvement in your financial journey. By analyzing what triggered disagreements and identifying patterns in your responses, you can proactively address potential conflicts before they escalate. Learning from past experiences allows you to navigate future discussions with a greater understanding of each other's perspectives and emotions.

Implementing strategies to prevent future disagreements involves open communication, setting clear boundaries, and cultivating a shared vision for your financial future. By establishing mutual goals and priorities, you create a sense of unity and purpose in your money management discussions. Remember to communicate openly and honestly, respecting each other's viewpoints and finding common ground to move forward constructively.

By focusing on constructive communication and problem-solving, you can strengthen your financial unity and build a stronger foundation for your relationship. Celebrate your progress, no matter how small, as each step forward brings you closer to your shared financial goals. Embrace the growth and learning opportunities that arise from overcoming challenges together, knowing that your partnership is resilient and capable of navigating any financial obstacle that comes your way.

Celebrating Progress and Growth:

As you reflect on the journey you and your partner have taken to overcome financial differences, it's essential to pause and celebrate the progress you've made. Recognize the growth in your relationship and the positive changes you've implemented in your approach to money management.

Take time to acknowledge the small victories along the way, whether it's sticking to a budget for a month, reaching a savings goal, or successfully navigating a challenging financial conversation. These milestones may seem insignificant on their own, but collectively, they represent a significant shift towards a more harmonious and united financial partnership.

Celebrate your progress by treating yourselves to a special dinner, planning a weekend getaway, or indulging in a shared experience that reinforces the bond you've forged through your financial journey. Use this time to express gratitude for each other's efforts and commitment to working together towards a common goal.

As you bask in the glow of your achievements, remember that celebrating progress is not just about the destination but also about the journey. Embrace the learning experiences, the challenges overcome, and the strengthened connection that arises from facing financial differences head-on. By celebrating your progress and growth, you affirm your resilience as a couple and set the stage for continued success in your financial journey together.

- Reinforcing the bond and teamwork achieved through overcoming financial differences.

Celebrating Progress and Growth:

As you reflect on the journey you and your partner have taken to overcome financial differences, take a moment to celebrate the growth and resilience you have shown. each challenge faced and resolved has strengthened the bond between you, solidifying your partnership in navigating the complexities of money management.

Through open communication and a shared commitment to understanding each other's perspectives, you have demonstrated an unwavering dedication to working together as a team. By acknowledging and addressing your differences constructively, you have fostered a deeper sense of trust and unity in your relationship.

In celebrating the progress you have made, take this opportunity to recognize the individual efforts and collective achievements that have brought you closer together. Whether it is reaching a milestone in your financial goals or successfully resolving a conflict, every step taken towards financial harmony is a testament to your shared vision and commitment to each other.

As you commemorate this moment of growth, remember to express gratitude to your partner for their contributions and support. By reinforcing the bond you have built through overcoming financial challenges, you strengthen the foundation of your relationship and pave the way for continued growth and prosperity together.

Working Together to Save and Invest

Setting Common Financial Goals

Discussing and aligning short-term and long-term financial objectives as a couple is a crucial step in building a strong financial foundation together. It requires open communication, mutual understanding, and a shared vision for the future. When setting common financial goals, it is important to consider both individual aspirations and collective dreams. Take the time to discuss your values, priorities, and expectations regarding money. Be honest and transparent about your financial situation, including income, expenses, debts, and savings. This will help you identify areas of alignment and potential areas of compromise. Start by outlining your short-term goals, such as saving for a vacation, buying a car, or paying off debt. Then, move on to discussing your long-term goals, such as buying a home, funding your children's education, or retiring comfortably. Consider the timeline for each goal, the amount of money needed, and the steps required to achieve it. Remember to prioritize your goals and focus on the ones that are most important to both of you. Setting common financial goals is not just about money; it is about building a life together and working towards a shared vision of success. By aligning your objectives and collaborating on a plan to achieve them, you can strengthen your relationship, enhance your financial well-being, and create a brighter future for yourselves as a couple.

- Discussing and aligning short-term and long-term financial objectives as a couple.

When discussing and aligning short-term and long-term financial objectives as a couple, it is crucial to focus on open communication and shared vision. Sit down with your partner to honestly assess your individual financial goals and aspirations. Share your dreams for the future and explore how your mutual financial objectives can align to create a strong foundation for your financial journey together. Consider factors such as saving for a home, starting a family, pursuing further education, or planning for retirement. By setting common financial goals, you can ensure that you are working together towards a shared vision of financial success. Take the time to listen to each other's perspectives, understand your priorities, and establish a roadmap that combines both short-term milestones and long-term achievements. Remember that clear communication and alignment on financial goals will not only strengthen your relationship but also pave the way for a more secure and prosperous future for both of you.

- Establishing priorities and timelines for savings and investments.

When it comes to establishing priorities and timelines for savings and investments as a couple, it is crucial to have open and honest discussions about your financial goals. By outlining clear priorities and setting realistic timelines, you can align your efforts towards building a secure financial future together.

Begin by identifying your short-term and long-term financial objectives as a couple. Determine what matters most to both of you and prioritize accordingly. Whether it's saving for a down payment on a house, planning for children's education, or building a retirement fund, clarity on your goals is essential.

Next, discuss the timelines associated with each goal. Consider factors such as your age, income level, and risk tolerance when setting these timelines. Be realistic about how long it will take to achieve each goal and break them down into manageable milestones along the way.

Create a roadmap that outlines the steps needed to reach each financial goal within the specified timelines. This may involve setting monthly savings targets, researching investment opportunities, or committing to specific financial strategies. By establishing a clear plan of action, you can stay focused and motivated to achieve your goals together.

Regularly review and reassess your priorities and timelines as circumstances change. Life is unpredictable, and your financial goals may need to be adjusted accordingly. Stay flexible and be willing to adapt your plan as needed to stay on track towards financial success.

Remember, communication is key when it comes to establishing priorities and timelines for savings and investments as a couple. Keep each other informed and involved in the decision-making process to ensure that you are working towards a common financial future. By setting clear priorities and timelines together, you can build a strong foundation for achieving your financial goals as a team.

Creating a Joint Saving Strategy

Deepening your financial bond as a couple involves creating a unified saving strategy that integrates both partners' viewpoints and aspirations. By pooling your resources and aligning your saving goals, you can fortify your financial foundation and pave the way for a prosperous future. It's imperative to embark on this journey with a shared vision and a collaborative mindset to achieve mutual financial well-being.

The first step in crafting a joint saving strategy is to outline your collective priorities and establish clear timelines for achieving them. Take the time to discuss and prioritize your saving goals, whether they involve building an emergency fund, saving for a home, planning for your children's education, or preparing for retirement. By setting specific targets and allocating resources accordingly, you lay a solid groundwork for your saving endeavors.

Once you've identified your saving objectives, the next phase involves developing a savings plan that reflects both partners' financial contributions and responsibilities. This plan should outline how much each of you will contribute to your joint savings account regularly, as well as any individual saving goals you may have. By delineating these roles and commitments, you ensure that both partners are actively engaged in nurturing your financial growth.

Maintaining open communication about your saving strategy is essential to its success. Regularly review your progress toward your saving goals and discuss any adjustments that may be necessary. Be transparent about your financial circumstances, share any concerns or unexpected expenses that may arise, and work together to address them proactively. By fostering a culture of accountability and teamwork, you strengthen your financial unity and build a foundation of trust and understanding.

Remember that a joint saving strategy is a dynamic process that requires ongoing effort and cooperation. Stay attuned to changes in your financial situation, such as income variations or unforeseen expenses, and adjust your saving plan accordingly. By staying committed to your shared saving goals and maintaining open lines of communication, you can navigate financial challenges together and achieve your desired outcomes.

- Developing a shared savings plan that reflects both partners' contributions and responsibilities.

Effective financial management as a couple requires the establishment of a shared savings plan that reflects the financial contributions and responsibilities of both partners. By creating a comprehensive savings strategy together, you can align your financial goals, track your progress, and ensure that each partner has a clear understanding of their role in building your financial future.

Start by having open and honest discussions about your individual financial situations, including income, expenses, and existing savings. Take the time to understand each other's financial priorities and aspirations, and work together to determine how you can jointly contribute to your shared savings goals.

Once you have a clear picture of your financial landscape, outline specific savings targets that you both aim to achieve. Whether you are saving for a major purchase, an emergency fund, or long-term investments, setting concrete goals will provide you with a roadmap to track your progress and stay motivated along the way.

Consider creating a detailed savings plan that outlines each partner's contribution amounts, frequency of deposits, and designated savings accounts or investment vehicles. Clearly defining these parameters will help you stay organized and accountable to your savings strategy.

Regularly monitor your savings progress and make adjustments as needed to ensure that you are staying on track towards your goals. Schedule check-ins with your partner to review your savings plan, celebrate milestones reached, and address any challenges or obstacles that may arise.

By developing a shared savings plan that reflects both partners' contributions and responsibilities, you are not only strengthening your financial foundation but also fostering a sense of unity and collaboration in your approach to managing money as a couple. Together, you can build a secure financial future and achieve your shared dreams and aspirations.

- Setting specific savings targets and monitoring progress regularly.

Setting specific savings targets and monitoring progress regularly involves a disciplined approach to achieving your financial goals. As a couple, it is essential to establish clear and measurable savings objectives that align with your shared vision for the future. Begin by identifying specific targets for different areas of your finances, whether it be an emergency fund, a down payment for a home, or retirement savings.

Once you have set these savings targets, it is crucial to monitor your progress regularly. Create a system to track your savings contributions and measure them against your goals. This could involve setting up automatic transfers to your savings accounts, keeping detailed records of your expenses and savings, or utilizing budgeting tools and apps to stay on top of your financial progress.

Reviewing your savings goals and progress together allows you to assess whether you are on track to reach your targets or if adjustments need to be made. If you find that you are falling short of your savings goals, consider ways to increase your savings rate or reduce expenses to stay on course. On the other hand, if you are exceeding your savings targets, you may want to reassess and reallocate those funds towards other financial goals or investments.

By setting specific savings targets and monitoring your progress regularly, you are actively taking control of your financial future as a couple. This proactive approach not only helps you stay focused and motivated but also enables you to make informed decisions about your finances and adjust your strategies as needed. Remember, consistent effort and dedication to your savings goals will pave the way for a more secure and prosperous financial future together.

Understanding Investment Options

Exploring different investment vehicles such as stocks, bonds, mutual funds, and real estate can provide opportunities for growth and wealth accumulation. Each investment option carries its own set of risks and potential returns, requiring careful consideration and research before making decisions.

Stocks represent ownership in a company and offer the potential for capital appreciation through the company's growth and profitability. However, stock prices can be volatile, influenced by market trends and company performance.

Bonds, on the other hand, are debt securities issued by governments or corporations. They provide a fixed interest rate and return of principal at maturity, making them a more conservative investment option compared to stocks.

Mutual funds pool money from multiple investors to invest in a diversified portfolio of stocks, bonds, or other securities. This collective investment approach spreads risk and allows individual investors to access professional money management.

Real estate investment involves purchasing property with the expectation of generating rental income or capital appreciation. Real estate can provide a steady income stream and potential tax benefits, but it also requires active management and comes with property-specific risks.

Understanding the characteristics and risks of these investment options is essential for building a well-rounded investment portfolio. Diversification across asset classes can help mitigate risk and maximize returns over time. Consider your financial goals, risk tolerance, and investment timeline when selecting the right mix of investment vehicles to achieve your financial objectives.

- Exploring different investment vehicles such as stocks, bonds, mutual funds, and real estate.

Exploring different investment vehicles such as stocks, bonds, mutual funds, and real estate can provide couples with a myriad of opportunities to grow their wealth over time. Each investment option comes with its own set of risks and potential returns, requiring careful consideration and understanding before making any decisions.

Stocks, or shares of ownership in a company, offer the potential for high returns but also come with significant risks due to market volatility. Investing in individual stocks requires thorough research and monitoring to make informed decisions on when to buy or sell.

Bonds, on the other hand, are debt securities issued by governments or corporations. While bonds generally offer lower returns compared to stocks, they are considered less risky and can provide a steady income stream through interest payments.

Mutual funds pool money from multiple investors to invest in a diversified portfolio of stocks, bonds, or other securities. This diversification helps spread out risk and can be a more hands-off approach to investing for couples who prefer a professional money manager to make investment decisions on their behalf.

Real estate investing involves purchasing properties with the expectation of generating rental income or selling them for a profit. Real estate can provide both ongoing cash flow and potential equity appreciation over time, but it also requires careful management and maintenance.

Before diving into any investment vehicle, couples should assess their risk tolerance, investment goals, and time horizon to determine the most suitable options for their financial future. Seeking guidance from a financial advisor or conducting thorough research can help couples make well-informed investment decisions that align with their long-term financial objectives.

- Educating yourselves on the risks and potential returns associated with each investment option.

Understanding the risks and potential returns associated with different investment options is crucial for making informed decisions about your financial future. Each investment vehicle comes with its own set of risks and rewards, and it's important to educate yourselves about these factors before committing your hard-earned money.

Stocks, for example, offer the potential for high returns but also come with a higher level of risk due to market fluctuations. Understanding how to research and analyze stocks can help you mitigate this risk and make more strategic investment choices.

Bonds, on the other hand, are considered lower-risk investments compared to stocks. They provide a fixed income stream but may offer lower returns. Being aware of the different types of bonds available and how interest rate changes can impact their value is essential for managing bond investments effectively.

Mutual funds offer diversification by pooling money from multiple investors to invest in a variety of assets. They can be a convenient way to access a diversified portfolio managed by professionals, but it's important to understand the fees and performance history of mutual funds before investing.

Real estate investments can provide passive income through rental properties or potential appreciation in property value. However, they also come with risks such as property market fluctuations and maintenance costs. Learning about local market trends and property management can help you make sound real estate investment decisions.

By educating yourselves about the risks and potential returns associated with each investment option, you can make informed choices that align with your financial goals and risk tolerance. Take the time to research and understand the dynamics of different investment vehicles to build a well-rounded investment portfolio that suits your unique financial situation.

Diversifying Your Portfolio

Diversifying Your Portfolio

Building a diversified investment portfolio is crucial for any couple looking to mitigate risks and maximize returns. By spreading your investments across different asset classes, industries, and geographic regions, you can reduce the impact of market fluctuations on your overall portfolio performance.

Diversification is not just about spreading your money thinly across various investments; it's about strategically selecting a mix of assets that have low correlation with each other. This means that when one investment is down, another may be up, helping to balance out your overall returns.

Consider allocating your funds across a mix of stocks, bonds, real estate, and other asset classes based on your risk tolerance and investment goals. Different asset classes have varying levels of risk and return potential, so diversifying can help you weather market volatility and achieve more stable long-term growth.

Furthermore, within each asset class, consider diversifying further by investing in different industries or sectors. This can help protect your portfolio from sector-specific risks and ensure that you're not overly exposed to any single market segment.

Regularly review your portfolio and make adjustments as needed to maintain optimal diversification. As your financial goals change and market conditions evolve, rebalancing your portfolio can help keep your investments aligned with your objectives.

Remember, diversification is not a guarantee against losses, but it can help reduce your overall risk exposure and increase your chances of achieving your financial goals over the long term. By building a diversified investment portfolio together as a couple, you can create a solid foundation for a more secure financial future.

- Building a diversified investment portfolio to mitigate risks and maximize returns.

Diversifying your investment portfolio is a crucial strategy in managing risk and maximizing returns. By spreading your investments across different asset classes, industries, and geographical regions, you can reduce the impact of volatility in any one particular investment. This approach helps to smooth out fluctuations in your portfolio's performance and increase the likelihood of achieving your financial goals over the long term.

When building a diversified portfolio, consider including a mix of stocks, bonds, mutual funds, real estate, and other investment vehicles. Each asset class has its own risk and return characteristics, so by combining them in a thoughtful manner, you can create a well-balanced portfolio that aligns with your risk tolerance and investment objectives.

Furthermore, diversification can also enhance your portfolio's resilience to market changes and economic downturns. During times of volatility or uncertainty, having a diversified investment portfolio can help cushion the impact of losses in one area with gains in another, providing a level of stability and protection for your overall financial well-being.

It's important to regularly review and rebalance your diversified portfolio to ensure it remains aligned with your goals and risk tolerance. As your financial situation or market conditions change, adjustments may be necessary to maintain the desired level of diversification and maximize the potential for long-term growth.

In conclusion, building a diversified investment portfolio is a fundamental strategy for mitigating risks and optimizing returns in your investment journey. By carefully selecting a mix of assets and monitoring your portfolio's performance over time, you can position yourself for financial success and weather the ups and downs of the market with confidence.

- Balancing between conservative and aggressive investment strategies based on your risk tolerance.

Balancing between conservative and aggressive investment strategies based on your risk tolerance is a crucial aspect of building a resilient investment portfolio. Conservative investments, such as bonds or savings accounts, offer more stability but generally lower returns. On the other hand, aggressive investments, like stocks or real estate, have the potential for higher returns but come with greater volatility and risk.

It is essential for couples to have open and honest discussions about their risk tolerance levels and investment preferences. Understanding each other's comfort with risk can help you find a balanced approach that aligns with your financial goals. Some individuals may lean towards conservative strategies to prioritize capital preservation, while others may feel comfortable taking on more risk in pursuit of higher returns.

Balancing conservative and aggressive investments requires a thoughtful evaluation of your financial situation, goals, and time horizon. Consider diversifying your portfolio across different asset classes to spread risk and optimize returns. By allocating your investments based on your risk tolerance, you can create a portfolio that reflects your shared financial values and objectives.

Keep in mind that risk tolerance can change over time due to various factors such as market conditions, life events, and personal preferences. Regularly reassessing your risk tolerance and adjusting your investment strategy accordingly can help you navigate fluctuations in the market and stay on track towards achieving your financial goals. Remember, finding the right balance between conservative and aggressive investments is a continuous process that requires communication, patience, and a shared commitment to your financial future.

Discussing Risk Management

When it comes to managing risk in your investment and savings strategy, it is crucial to have open and honest discussions with your partner. By engaging in transparent conversations about risk management strategies, insurance coverage, and emergency funds, you can ensure that both individuals in the relationship are prepared for any financial challenges that may arise.

One key aspect of discussing risk management is assessing the level of insurance coverage you have in place. This includes health insurance, life insurance, disability insurance, and property and casualty insurance. Understanding the extent of your coverage and any potential gaps can help you feel more secure in the face of unexpected events.

In addition to insurance, building an emergency fund is a fundamental part of risk management. An emergency fund serves as a financial safety net, providing you with a cushion in case of job loss, medical emergencies, or other unforeseen circumstances. By setting aside a designated amount of money in an easily accessible account, you can safeguard against financial instability during tough times.

Moreover, discussing risk management should also involve planning for long-term financial goals, such as retirement. Considering factors like inflation, market volatility, and investment risks can help you make informed decisions about your savings and investment strategy. By factoring in these elements and continuously monitoring your portfolio, you can adjust your plan as needed to mitigate risks and maximize returns over time.

Overall, engaging in discussions about risk management with your partner can lead to a stronger financial foundation and greater peace of mind. By working together to assess your risk tolerance, insurance coverage, emergency funds, and long-term financial goals, you can build a comprehensive risk management strategy that protects your financial well-being and prepares you for whatever the future may hold.

- Having transparent discussions about risk management strategies, including insurance coverage and emergency funds.

Having transparent discussions about risk management strategies is essential for ensuring the financial security and stability of your partnership. By openly communicating about potential risks and uncertainties, you can proactively plan for unexpected events and minimize their impact on your savings and investments. One crucial aspect of risk management is assessing the adequacy of your insurance coverage. Whether it's health insurance, life insurance, disability insurance, or property and casualty insurance, having the right policies in place can provide you with a safety net in times of need.

Similarly, building an emergency fund is a fundamental risk management strategy that can help you weather financial storms. Setting aside a designated amount of money in a separate account for unforeseen expenses can prevent you from dipping into your savings or investments during emergencies. Your emergency fund should ideally cover three to six months' worth of essential living expenses to safeguard your financial well-being.

Furthermore, discussing the potential risks associated with your investment portfolio is crucial for managing your overall financial risk. Understanding the volatility and potential losses associated with different asset classes can help you make informed decisions about diversification and asset allocation. By assessing your risk tolerance and investment objectives, you can construct a well-balanced portfolio that aligns with your financial goals.

In conclusion, open and transparent discussions about risk management strategies, including insurance coverage and emergency funds, are vital components of a comprehensive financial plan. By addressing potential risks proactively and collaboratively, you can protect your financial future and navigate unexpected challenges with confidence.

- Planning for unexpected financial challenges and how they may impact your savings and investments.

Understanding the potential impact of unexpected financial challenges on your savings and investments is crucial for long-term financial security. Life is unpredictable, and various situations, such as job loss, medical emergencies, or sudden expenses, can arise when least expected. These situations can have a significant effect on your financial plans if not properly prepared for.

It is essential to proactively plan for unexpected financial challenges by establishing emergency funds. An emergency fund serves as a safety net, providing liquidity to cover sudden expenses or income loss without having to dip into your savings or investments. Aim to set aside at least three to six months' worth of living expenses in your emergency fund to ensure you are prepared for unforeseen circumstances.

In addition to having an emergency fund, consider the role of insurance in managing financial risks. Health insurance, disability insurance, life insurance, and property insurance can protect you and your assets in case of unexpected events. Reviewing your insurance coverage regularly and ensuring it aligns with your current financial situation and needs is essential for comprehensive risk management.

When unexpected financial challenges do arise, it is crucial to assess their impact on your savings and investments promptly. Evaluate the extent of the financial setback, reassess your financial goals, and adjust your savings and investment strategies accordingly. Depending on the nature of the challenge, you may need to reallocate funds, pause certain investments, or explore alternative sources of income to weather the storm.

Communication is key when navigating unexpected financial challenges as a couple. Keep an open and honest dialogue about the situation, share concerns and ideas for solutions, and work together to address the challenges effectively. By facing unexpected financial difficulties as a team, you can strengthen your financial resilience and emerge stronger from the experience. Remember that setbacks are a normal part of financial planning, and how you respond to them can ultimately shape your financial future.

Monitoring and Adjusting Investments

To effectively monitor and adjust your investments, it is crucial to regularly assess the performance of your portfolio. This ongoing evaluation allows you to identify any fluctuations or trends that may impact your financial goals. Start by reviewing your investment holdings to ensure they align with your overall financial objectives.

Evaluate the performance of each investment against benchmarks and industry standards to gauge its effectiveness.

Additionally, stay informed about market conditions and economic trends that could influence your investment portfolio. Keep abreast of relevant news and updates in the financial world to make informed decisions about rebalancing your investments. Consider consulting with a financial advisor to gain expert insights and recommendations on adjusting your portfolio strategically.

When adjusting your investments, take a diligent and calculated approach. Avoid making impulsive decisions based on short-term market fluctuations. Instead, assess the long-term viability of your investments and consider the potential impact of adjustments on your overall financial plan. Be proactive in reallocating assets based on your risk tolerance, investment goals, and changing market conditions.

Furthermore, document and track the changes you make to your investment portfolio. Maintain detailed records of adjustments, including the rationale behind each decision and the anticipated outcomes. Tracking your investment adjustments over time provides valuable insights into the effectiveness of your investment strategy and helps you make informed decisions in the future.

In conclusion, monitoring and adjusting your investments is a continuous process that requires attentiveness, analysis, and strategic decision-making. By staying proactive and informed about your investments, you can optimize your portfolio to better align with your financial goals and navigate changing market dynamics effectively. Regular review and adjustment of your investments are essential components of a successful long-term investment strategy.

- Regularly reviewing the performance of your investments and adjusting your portfolio as needed.

Regularly reviewing the performance of your investments is a critical aspect of financial management. It allows you to track the progress of your portfolio, assess its performance against your financial goals, and make necessary adjustments to ensure your investments are on the right track. By monitoring your investments regularly, you can identify any underperforming assets, capitalize on opportunities for growth, and align your portfolio with your risk tolerance and investment objectives.

When reviewing your investments, it's essential to consider factors such as market trends, economic conditions, and fluctuations in asset values. By staying informed about the financial markets and understanding how external factors can impact your investments, you can make informed decisions about when to buy, sell, or hold onto specific assets. Additionally, monitoring the performance of your investments allows you to assess whether your current investment strategy is aligned with your long-term financial goals or if adjustments are needed to optimize returns and mitigate risks.

One way to track the performance of your investments is to regularly review your portfolio's asset allocation. Ensure that your investments are diversified across different asset classes to spread risk and maximize returns. Evaluate the performance of individual assets within your portfolio and consider rebalancing your investments periodically to maintain your desired asset allocation.

Another key aspect of monitoring your investments is assessing the fees and expenses associated with your investment accounts. High fees can eat into your returns over time, so it's essential to review the costs of your investments and explore more cost-effective options when appropriate. By minimizing unnecessary expenses, you can potentially increase your overall investment returns and improve the efficiency of your portfolio.

In addition to tracking the performance of your investments on your own, seeking professional advice from a financial advisor can provide valuable insights and expertise. A financial advisor can offer personalized investment recommendations, help you navigate complex financial markets, and develop a tailored investment strategy that aligns with your risk tolerance and financial goals.

Working with a financial advisor can also provide you with peace of mind knowing that your investments are being managed by a knowledgeable professional who has your best interests in mind.

- Seeking professional advice from a financial advisor to optimize your investment strategy.

When it comes to optimizing your investment strategy, seeking professional advice from a financial advisor can be a crucial step in ensuring that your financial goals are on track. A financial advisor has the expertise and knowledge to provide personalized guidance based on your unique financial situation, risk tolerance, and long-term objectives.

Financial advisors can help you assess the performance of your current investments and determine if any adjustments are needed to align with your goals. By analyzing market trends, economic indicators, and your portfolio's performance, a financial advisor can offer valuable insights on potential opportunities for growth and risk mitigation.

Additionally, a financial advisor can assist you in diversifying your investment portfolio effectively, balancing between different asset classes to optimize returns while managing risks. They can recommend suitable investment options based on your investment horizon, financial goals, and tolerance for risk.

Moreover, a financial advisor can provide guidance on tax-efficient investment strategies, helping you minimize tax liabilities and maximize after-tax returns. They can also offer advice on retirement savings vehicles such as IRAs and 401(k) plans, ensuring that you are taking full advantage of tax incentives and employer matching contributions.

Ultimately, working with a financial advisor can give you peace of mind knowing that your investment strategy is aligned with your financial goals and risk tolerance. Their expertise and objective perspective can help you make informed decisions to build and preserve wealth over the long term, enhancing your financial security and well-being.

Contributing to Retirement Accounts

Planning for retirement is a crucial aspect of securing your financial future. Contributing to retirement accounts, such as Individual Retirement Accounts (IRAs) or employer-sponsored retirement plans, is a proactive step towards building a nest egg for your golden years.

By setting aside a portion of your income into retirement accounts, you are investing in your future self. These accounts offer tax advantages and potential growth on your contributions over time. It's important to understand the different types of retirement accounts available to you and choose the ones that align with your financial goals and risk tolerance.

Consulting with a financial advisor can help you optimize your retirement savings strategy. They can provide valuable insights on asset allocation, risk management, and investment diversification tailored to your specific circumstances. A financial advisor can also assist you in maximizing employer matching contributions and taking advantage of any available tax benefits related to retirement savings.

Regularly contributing to retirement accounts not only helps you build a financial cushion for retirement but also instills discipline in your savings habits. It's essential to establish a consistent savings routine and monitor the performance of your retirement accounts to ensure you are on track to meet your retirement goals.

Planning for retirement as a couple allows you to align your financial objectives and work towards a shared future. By contributing to retirement accounts together, you are pooling your resources and building a secure foundation for the years ahead. Start by discussing your retirement goals and creating a savings plan that reflects your aspirations and lifestyle preferences. Together, you can navigate the complexities of retirement planning and take proactive steps towards a financially comfortable retirement.

- Planning for retirement together by contributing to individual retirement accounts (IRAs) or employer-sponsored retirement plans.

When planning for retirement together, it is essential to prioritize contributing to individual retirement accounts (IRAs) or employer-sponsored retirement plans. These accounts serve as valuable tools to help you build a financial cushion for your post-career years. By making regular contributions to these accounts, you are setting yourselves up for a more secure and comfortable retirement.

IRAs offer tax advantages that can help your retirement savings grow more effectively over time. Depending on the type of IRA you choose, you may benefit from tax-deferred growth or tax-free withdrawals in retirement. By contributing to IRAs, you are not only saving for the future but also potentially reducing your current tax burden.

Employer-sponsored retirement plans, such as 401(k) or 403(b) accounts, often come with additional benefits, such as employer matching contributions. This means that your employer will match a portion of your contributions, effectively boosting your retirement savings without any additional effort on your part. Taking full advantage of employer matches can significantly accelerate the growth of your retirement nest egg.

By diligently contributing to both IRAs and employer-sponsored plans, you are laying a strong foundation for your retirement years. These accounts give you the opportunity to invest in a diversified portfolio of assets, allowing your savings to grow over time. Regular contributions and a long-term perspective are key to maximizing the benefits of these retirement vehicles.

As you plan for retirement together, consider your joint financial goals and how your contributions to retirement accounts align with these objectives. Monitor your accounts regularly to track progress toward your retirement savings targets and make adjustments as needed. By working together to build your retirement nest egg through IRAs and employer-sponsored plans, you are taking proactive steps to ensure a financially secure future for both of you.

- Maximizing tax advantages and employer matching contributions to build your retirement nest egg.

Maximizing tax advantages and employer matching contributions to build your retirement nest egg is a crucial aspect of securing your financial future. By taking advantage of tax-deferred retirement accounts such as IRAs or participating in employer-sponsored retirement plans, you can grow your retirement savings more efficiently.

Contributing to these accounts not only helps you save for retirement but also provides tax benefits. Traditional IRAs and employer-sponsored plans like 401(k)s allow you to reduce your taxable income in the current year, lowering your tax liability. This tax deferral can result in significant savings over time as your investments grow tax-free until withdrawal during retirement.

In addition to maximizing tax advantages, leveraging employer matching contributions can significantly boost your retirement savings. Many employers offer matching contributions to their employees' retirement accounts, typically up to a certain percentage of the employee's salary. By contributing enough to receive the full employer match, you are essentially getting free money added to your retirement fund.

To make the most of these opportunities, it's essential to contribute the maximum allowed amount to your retirement accounts each year. By taking advantage of both tax benefits and employer matches, you can accelerate the growth of your retirement nest egg and ensure a more financially secure future for you and your partner. Remember, the key to building a solid foundation for retirement is to start early, contribute consistently, and prioritize maximizing these valuable benefits.

Saving for Major Life Events

Saving for Major Life Events

Life is a series of milestones that shape our journey and define our future. Whether it's buying a home, starting a family, or pursuing further education, these major life events often come with significant financial implications. Planning and saving strategically for these milestones are essential to ensure that you can navigate these transitions with confidence and security.

When it comes to buying a home, it's important to consider not just the initial down payment but also ongoing mortgage payments, property taxes, and maintenance costs. Saving diligently towards this goal allows you to approach the homebuying process with financial stability and peace of mind.

Starting a family is a joyous occasion, but it also requires careful financial planning. From prenatal care to childcare expenses, raising a child comes with a range of costs that need to be factored into your budget. Saving for these expenses in advance can help alleviate the financial stress that often accompanies the arrival of a new family member.

For those considering further education or career advancement, saving for tuition, books, and other related expenses is crucial. Whether it's pursuing a degree, certification, or professional development courses, investing in your education can yield long-term benefits for your career and financial future.

By proactively saving for these major life events, you can approach them with confidence and preparedness. Building a financial cushion for these milestones not only helps you cover the associated costs but also allows you to focus on enjoying these significant moments without being overwhelmed by financial stress. Remember, saving for major life events is not just about money—it's about investing in your future and creating a solid foundation for the life you envision for yourself and your loved ones.

- Saving strategically for major life events such as buying a home, starting a family, or pursuing further education.

Saving strategically for major life events such as buying a home, starting a family, or pursuing further education requires careful planning and discipline. These significant milestones in life come with financial implications that can impact your overall savings and investment plan. By setting specific goals and timelines for each major event, you can proactively work towards achieving them while maintaining financial stability.

When saving for a home, consider factors such as the down payment, closing costs, and ongoing mortgage payments. Calculate how much you need to save each month to reach your target amount within your desired timeframe. Research various mortgage options and interest rates to determine the most suitable financing plan for your home purchase.

Starting a family involves additional expenses such as childcare, healthcare, and education costs. Create a budget that accounts for these new financial responsibilities and adjust your savings plan accordingly. Explore opportunities to invest in college savings plans or other education funds to prepare for your children's future educational needs.

If you are considering further education for yourself or your partner, factor in tuition fees, living expenses, and potential loss of income during the study period. Evaluate the return on investment of pursuing additional qualifications and how it aligns with your long-term financial goals. Explore scholarship opportunities, student loans, or employer-sponsored educational benefits to help fund your educational pursuits.

By saving strategically for these major life events, you can ensure that you are financially prepared to navigate these transitions smoothly. Communicate openly with your partner about your shared financial goals and work together to prioritize saving for these milestones. Remember to adjust your savings and investment plan as needed to accommodate changing circumstances and opportunities that may arise along the way.

- Discussing the financial implications of these events and how they fit into your overall savings and investment plan.

Planning for major life events such as buying a home, starting a family, or pursuing further education requires careful consideration of the financial implications involved. These events represent significant milestones in your life that can have a lasting impact on your financial well-being. It is essential to evaluate how these events align with your overall savings and investment plan to ensure that you are financially prepared for the future.

When discussing the financial implications of these events, it is crucial to take into account your current financial situation, goals, and timelines. Assessing your savings and investment plans can help you determine how these major life events fit into your broader financial strategy. Consider how achieving these milestones may impact your cash flow, savings goals, and long-term financial objectives.

For instance, buying a home involves substantial upfront costs such as down payment, closing costs, and ongoing expenses like mortgage payments, property taxes, and maintenance. This purchase will likely impact your budget and savings goals, requiring adjustments to accommodate these new financial responsibilities. Evaluating how homeownership fits into your savings and investment plan can help you make informed decisions and prepare for this significant financial commitment.

Similarly, starting a family or pursuing further education can also have significant financial implications. These life events may require additional expenses for childcare, education, healthcare, or tuition fees. Understanding how these costs will affect your financial resources can help you plan accordingly and prioritize your savings and investment goals. By incorporating these considerations into your overall financial plan, you can ensure that you are adequately prepared for the financial impact of these major life events.

Discussing the financial implications of these events as a couple allows you to align your priorities, assess your readiness, and make informed decisions about your financial future. By openly communicating about your savings and investment goals in the context of these major life events, you can work together to create a solid financial foundation that supports your aspirations and aspirations.

Celebrating Financial Milestones

As a couple, you have worked diligently to stay committed to your joint savings and investment plan. You have navigated financial challenges and celebrated small victories along the way. Now, it's time to pause and acknowledge the significant milestones you have achieved together.

Reaching a financial milestone is not just about the numbers on paper; it represents your shared dedication, discipline, and perseverance. It is a testament to your ability to work as a team, communicate effectively, and make sound financial decisions together.

Take a moment to reflect on how far you have come since you first started this journey. Whether it's reaching a specific savings target, seeing your investment portfolio grow, or paying off a significant amount of debt, each milestone is a stepping stone towards your larger financial goals.

Celebrating these milestones can be a powerful motivator to keep pushing forward and stay committed to your financial plan. It's essential to acknowledge and appreciate the progress you have made, no matter how big or small.

Consider commemorating these achievements in a meaningful way that resonates with both of you. Whether it's a special dinner, a weekend getaway, or simply taking the time to express gratitude for each other's efforts, celebrating together strengthens your bond and reinforces your shared commitment to financial success.

Remember, celebrating financial milestones is not just about the present moment; it's also about setting the stage for future success. Use these celebratory moments as opportunities to reassess your goals, reevaluate your strategies, and set new milestones to strive towards as a couple.

By recognizing and celebrating your financial milestones, you not only validate your hard work but also solidify your partnership in managing your finances. Together, you can continue to achieve great things and build a secure financial future for yourselves.

- Acknowledging and celebrating reaching savings and investment milestones as a couple.

As you achieve significant savings and investment milestones together, it is essential to take a moment to acknowledge and celebrate these accomplishments. These milestones are a testament to your shared dedication, discipline, and financial teamwork. Reflect on the journey that led you to this milestone and the sacrifices made along the way. Pause to appreciate the progress you have made towards your joint financial goals and the positive impact it has on your future together.

Celebrating these milestones can strengthen your bond as a couple and reaffirm your commitment to your financial well-being. Whether it's reaching a specific savings target, seeing your investment portfolio grow, or achieving a significant return on your investments, each milestone represents a stepping stone towards your shared financial future. Take the time to acknowledge the hard work and dedication that went into achieving these milestones and the resilience you displayed in overcoming any obstacles along the way.

Celebrate in a way that is meaningful to both of you, whether it's a special dinner, a weekend getaway, or simply sharing a moment of gratitude and reflection together. Use this opportunity to express appreciation for each other's contributions to your financial journey and reinforce your shared vision for the future. By acknowledging and celebrating these milestones as a couple, you not only celebrate your financial success but also reaffirm your partnership and commitment to building a secure and prosperous future together.

- Reflecting on your progress and setting new goals to continue building your financial future together.

As you reflect on your financial journey together, take pride in the milestones you have achieved thus far. Celebrate the discipline and dedication that have brought you closer to your shared goals. Embrace the moments of triumph, both big and small, as they symbolize your commitment to each other and your financial future.

Now, look ahead with clarity and purpose. Set new goals that inspire and challenge you to reach greater heights. Consider what you have learned along the way and how you can leverage that knowledge to propel yourselves forward. Define your ambitions together, mapping out a roadmap that will guide your actions and decisions in the days and years to come.

Be intentional in your goal-setting process. Ensure that your new objectives are specific, measurable, achievable, relevant, and time-bound. By establishing clear targets, you provide yourselves with a framework for success and accountability. Discuss your aspirations openly and honestly, aligning your individual desires to create a unified vision for your financial future.

As you embark on this next chapter of your financial journey, remember the importance of communication and collaboration. Engage in regular conversations about your progress and challenges, offering support and encouragement to one another. Embrace the opportunity to grow together, learning from each other's strengths and weaknesses as you navigate the complexities of wealth-building as a team.

With each new goal you set and achieve, you solidify your bond and lay a foundation for lasting financial security and prosperity. Embrace the process of continual improvement, knowing that growth is not only measured in dollars and cents but also in the strength of your partnership and the depth of your shared dreams. Keep moving forward, hand in hand, towards a future filled with promise and possibility.

Continuing Financial Education and Growth

As you continue your journey towards financial independence and wealth-building, committing to ongoing financial education and growth is imperative. The world of finance is constantly evolving, and staying up-to-date with the latest trends, strategies, and tools is essential for maximizing your savings and investment potential.

One way to enhance your financial knowledge is by engaging in continuous learning opportunities. Consider enrolling in workshops, seminars, or online courses that focus on personal finance, investment strategies, and financial planning. By dedicating time and effort to expand your financial literacy, you can make more informed decisions about your money and achieve your financial goals more effectively.

In addition to formal education, take advantage of resources such as financial websites, blogs, podcasts, and books that offer valuable insights and practical tips for managing your finances. Joining financial discussion groups or online forums can also provide you with a platform to exchange ideas, seek advice, and learn from the experiences of others in the financial community.

Furthermore, consulting with a financial advisor can offer personalized guidance tailored to your specific financial situation and goals. A professional advisor can help you navigate complex financial matters, optimize your investment portfolio, and develop a comprehensive financial plan that aligns with your objectives.

Remember, financial education is a lifelong process that requires dedication and a willingness to adapt to changing circumstances. By prioritizing continuous learning and growth in your financial journey, you are equipping yourselves with the knowledge and skills needed to secure your financial future and achieve lasting prosperity.

- Committing to ongoing financial education and learning opportunities to enhance your savings and investment knowledge.

By committing to ongoing financial education and learning opportunities, you are investing in your future financial success. The world of finance is constantly evolving, and staying informed is crucial to making informed decisions about your savings and investments. Take advantage of online resources, books, workshops, and courses to expand your knowledge and skills in financial management. Engage in discussions with experts, attend seminars, and seek mentorship to gain valuable insights into the ever-changing landscape of personal finance. By continuously educating yourself, you can enhance your ability to make strategic financial decisions and grow your savings and investment portfolio over time.

- Encouraging each other to stay informed and make informed decisions for your financial well-being.

Encouraging each other to stay informed and make informed decisions for your financial well-being can be a crucial aspect of your journey towards financial success. As partners in both life and finances, it is essential to support and uplift each other in staying knowledgeable about the ever-evolving world of money management. By sharing valuable resources, attending financial workshops or seminars together, and engaging in open discussions about financial news and trends, you can deepen your understanding and make more informed decisions regarding your financial future.

Remember, the more you empower each other with information and education, the better equipped you will be to navigate the complexities of personal finance and achieve your shared goals. So, make a commitment to prioritize financial education and encourage each other to take proactive steps towards securing your financial well-being.

Planning for Big Financial Decisions Together

Understanding the Importance of Strategic Financial Planning

Strategic financial planning is the cornerstone of a successful and sustainable financial future for any couple. It involves setting clear objectives, outlining detailed action plans, and making informed decisions to achieve long-term financial stability and security. By taking a proactive and deliberate approach to managing your finances, you can align your financial goals with your values and aspirations as a couple, paving the way for a brighter and more secure future together.

Effective strategic financial planning requires a deep understanding of your current financial situation, including your income, expenses, assets, and liabilities. By conducting a thorough analysis of your financial landscape, you can identify areas for improvement, set realistic goals, and develop a roadmap for achieving them. This process lays the foundation for building a strong financial foundation and enables you to make informed decisions that support your long-term financial well-being.

Strategic financial planning also involves looking beyond the present moment and considering the future implications of your financial choices. By setting long-term financial goals as a couple, you can create a shared vision for your financial future and work towards achieving milestones that are meaningful to both of you. Whether your goals include buying a home, starting a family, saving for retirement, or pursuing a dream vacation, strategic financial planning helps you prioritize your objectives and allocate resources effectively to achieve them.

Furthermore, strategic financial planning empowers you to anticipate and navigate potential challenges and opportunities that may arise along the way. By developing contingency plans and alternative scenarios, you can adapt to changing circumstances and make sound financial decisions that align with your overarching goals. This proactive approach to financial planning not only enhances your financial resilience but also strengthens your ability to weather unexpected setbacks and capitalize on new opportunities as they emerge.

In essence, understanding the importance of strategic financial planning is essential for couples who seek to build a secure financial future together. By embracing this holistic and forward-thinking approach to managing your finances, you can align your financial goals, values, and aspirations with a clear roadmap for success. Strategic financial planning is not just about numbers; it's about creating a shared vision for your future and taking deliberate steps to turn that vision into reality.

Setting Long-Term Financial Goals as a Couple

As a couple embarking on a financial journey together, setting long-term financial goals is a crucial step towards securing your future and achieving your shared dreams. These goals serve as guiding beacons, illuminating the path you both wish to tread upon as you navigate the complexities of financial planning.

When setting long-term financial goals, it is essential to engage in deep and meaningful conversations with your partner. Take the time to explore your individual values, aspirations, and financial priorities. By aligning your visions and creating a unified roadmap, you can establish a solid foundation for your joint financial endeavors.

Consider the various aspects of your life that may be impacted by your financial goals. From purchasing a home to starting a family, retiring comfortably, or traveling the world together, envision the life you wish to build as a couple. By clearly defining these long-term objectives, you can motivate each other and stay focused on your collective financial aspirations.

In setting long-term financial goals, it is imperative to be realistic and specific. Break down your overarching objectives into smaller, achievable milestones that can be measured and tracked over time. By doing so, you can monitor your progress, celebrate your successes, and make adjustments as needed to stay on course towards realizing your shared financial dreams.

Furthermore, consider the timeframe within which you aim to achieve these long-term financial goals. Whether it be in five, ten, or twenty years, establishing a timeline can provide a sense of urgency and structure to your planning efforts. Remember that flexibility is key, as life may present unexpected opportunities or challenges along the way.

Ultimately, setting long-term financial goals as a couple is a testament to your commitment to each other and your future together. By sharing a vision, communicating openly, and working collaboratively towards your financial objectives, you can lay the groundwork for a secure and prosperous life ahead.

Conducting Thorough Research and Analysis for Major Financial Decisions

Conducting thorough research and analysis for major financial decisions is crucial for ensuring the long-term financial stability and success of a couple. It requires a methodical and diligent approach to gather all necessary information, assess various factors, and make informed choices that align with your shared goals.

Begin by defining the specific financial decision at hand and clearly outlining the objectives you hope to achieve. This could involve major purchases, investments, career changes, or other significant financial commitments that will impact your future together.

Next, gather relevant data and information from reputable sources to enhance your understanding of the decision-making process. Consider factors such as market trends, potential risks, regulatory requirements, and economic conditions that may influence the outcomes of your choices.

Analyze the data systematically, taking into account both quantitative and qualitative aspects of the decision. Utilize financial tools, models, and projections to evaluate different scenarios and anticipate potential outcomes. This analytical approach will help you make well-informed decisions based on a thorough understanding of the risks and rewards involved.

Consult with financial experts or professionals to gain additional insights and perspectives on the decision at hand. Their expertise and experience can provide valuable guidance and help you navigate complex financial considerations with confidence.

Consider the long-term implications of the decision on your financial well-being and relationship dynamics. Evaluate how this decision aligns with your shared values, goals, and aspirations as a couple. Reflect on the potential impacts on your financial future and determine whether the decision supports your collective vision for the years ahead.

By conducting thorough research and analysis for major financial decisions, you empower yourselves to make informed choices that enhance your financial security and strengthen your partnership. Approach each decision with care, diligence, and a commitment to building a solid financial foundation for your future together.

Considering the Risks and Rewards Involved in Financial Choices

It is crucial for couples to carefully weigh the risks and rewards involved in major financial decisions. Every financial choice has the potential to impact your present and future financial well-being. By considering the potential risks and rewards, you can make informed decisions that align with your goals and values.

When evaluating financial choices, it is essential to assess the potential risks involved. Factors such as market volatility, economic conditions, and regulatory changes can all influence the outcome of your decisions. By conducting a thorough risk analysis, you can anticipate potential challenges and develop strategies to mitigate them.

On the other hand, every financial decision also presents rewards that can enhance your financial standing. Whether it's the potential for financial growth, increased stability, or achieving a major life goal, identifying and understanding the rewards can motivate and guide your decision-making process.

It is important to weigh the risks against the rewards and consider the trade-offs involved in each financial choice. By carefully evaluating the potential outcomes and aligning them with your long-term goals, you can make decisions that are strategic, thoughtful, and beneficial for your financial future.

Remember, taking calculated risks can lead to great rewards, but it is essential to approach financial decisions with caution and foresight. By considering the risks and rewards involved in each choice, you can navigate financial challenges with confidence and make decisions that will set you on the path to financial success.

Seeking Professional Advice and Expert Opinion when Necessary

Seeking professional advice and expert opinion when necessary is a crucial step in making big financial decisions as a couple. Financial matters can be complex and overwhelming, and having the guidance of a knowledgeable professional can provide invaluable insight and clarity. Whether it's consulting with a financial advisor, accountant, or lawyer, seeking expert advice can help you navigate through the intricacies of financial planning.

A professional advisor can offer you specialized knowledge and expertise that may not be readily available to you. They can provide objective analysis of your financial situation, offer personalized recommendations tailored to your specific needs, and help you understand the potential risks and rewards associated with different financial choices. By tapping into their expertise, you can make more informed decisions that align with your long-term goals and aspirations.

Moreover, seeking professional advice can help you avoid common pitfalls and mistakes that couples often encounter when making big financial decisions. Professionals can help you identify blind spots, challenge your assumptions, and offer alternative perspectives that you may not have considered. They can also provide a level of objectivity that may be difficult to maintain when emotions are running high.

Furthermore, involving a professional advisor can strengthen your relationship as a couple. It demonstrates a commitment to working together to secure your financial future and shows that you value each other's opinions and well-being. By embracing expert advice, you can foster trust, open communication, and collaboration in your decision-making process, ultimately strengthening your bond as a team.

In conclusion, seeking professional advice and expert opinion when necessary is a wise and proactive approach to making big financial decisions as a couple. It empowers you with the knowledge and insights needed to navigate complex financial landscapes, avoid potential pitfalls, and strengthen your relationship through shared decision-making and collaboration.

Evaluating the Impact of Big Financial Decisions on Your Relationship

Evaluating the Impact of Big Financial Decisions on Your Relationship

Making significant financial decisions can have a profound impact on the dynamics and stability of a relationship. It is essential to recognize that these decisions go beyond mere numbers and investments; they often reflect underlying values, priorities, and communication patterns within the partnership.

Before embarking on major financial choices, take the time to consider how they may affect your relationship. Will this decision align with both partners' goals and aspirations? Will it create feelings of equity and fairness in how resources are allocated? Understanding these potential implications can help avoid misunderstandings and conflicts down the road.

Moreover, big financial decisions have the power to strengthen or strain a relationship's trust. Transparency, honesty, and open communication are crucial during the evaluation process. Ensure that both partners are actively involved in the decision-making and fully understand the implications of the choices being made.

Furthermore, consider the long-term consequences of the decision on your relationship. Will it bring you closer together or create rifts and resentments? Reflect on how the decision aligns with your shared values and vision for the future. It is essential to approach these decisions with a sense of unity and collaboration, rather than individual agendas.

Ultimately, evaluating the impact of big financial decisions on your relationship requires empathy, understanding, and a shared commitment to navigate challenges together. By proactively addressing potential concerns and discussing the emotional and relational aspects of the choices at hand, you can foster a stronger and more resilient partnership built on trust and mutual respect.

Creating a Decision-Making Process that Aligns with Your Shared Values

Making major financial decisions as a couple requires a thoughtful and aligned approach that integrates both partners' values and beliefs. By creating a decision-making process that resonates with your shared values, you can ensure that your choices reflect your joint priorities and aspirations.

Begin by discussing and identifying the core values that shape your financial decisions as a couple. Consider what matters most to both of you in terms of money, relationships, and life goals. Understanding these values will serve as a compass for guiding your decision-making process.

Next, establish clear and open communication channels to facilitate discussions about financial choices. Encourage each other to express viewpoints and concerns without judgment, and actively listen to one another's perspectives. This mutual respect and understanding will foster a collaborative decision-making environment.

When facing major financial decisions, evaluate how each option aligns with your shared values and long-term goals. Consider the potential impact on your relationship, financial stability, and overall well-being. Assess whether the decision reflects your joint vision and enhances your collective future.

Take into account any potential trade-offs or sacrifices that may arise from the decision. Discuss how each choice resonates with your values and priorities as a couple, and weigh the benefits and drawbacks of each option accordingly. Strive to find a balance that honors your shared values while optimizing the outcome for both partners.

Lastly, document your decision-making process and the rationale behind your choices. Keep a record of the factors considered, the values upheld, and the agreements reached. This not only ensures transparency and clarity but also serves as a reference point for future financial decisions and discussions.

By creating a decision-making process that aligns with your shared values, you can navigate major financial choices as a couple with confidence and unity. This deliberate and intentional approach will strengthen your relationship, reinforce your bond, and pave the way for a financially secure and fulfilling future together.

Managing Emotions and Stress during the Planning Phase

Managing Emotions and Stress during the Planning Phase

One of the most challenging aspects of tackling big financial decisions as a couple is managing the emotions and stress that inevitably arise during the planning phase. Money is a sensitive topic that can trigger a range of feelings, including anxiety, fear, frustration, and even resentment. It's crucial to recognize and address these emotions constructively to ensure that they don't derail the decision-making process.

As you navigate the complexities of financial planning together, it's essential to maintain open communication and a sense of mutual respect. Listen actively to each other's concerns and perspectives without judgment, and validate each other's feelings, even if you don't necessarily agree. Acknowledge the emotions that arise and work together to address them as a team.

Establishing a supportive environment built on trust and understanding can help alleviate some of the stress associated with making big financial decisions. Create a safe space where both partners feel comfortable expressing their thoughts and emotions without fear of criticism or backlash. Remember that you're a team, and your goal is to work collaboratively towards a shared vision of your financial future.

Practice mindfulness and self-awareness during the planning phase to stay grounded and focused. Take breaks when needed to recharge and regain perspective. Engage in stress-relieving activities together, whether it's going for a walk, practicing meditation, or simply taking a moment to breathe deeply. Prioritize self-care and well-being to ensure that you're in the right mindset to tackle complex financial decisions as a couple.

Lastly, remember that it's okay to seek outside support if the emotions and stress become overwhelming. Consider consulting a financial planner, therapist, or counselor to help you navigate the emotional challenges that may arise during the planning phase. By proactively managing your emotions and stress, you can approach big financial decisions with clarity, resilience, and unity as a couple.

Developing Contingency Plans for Unexpected Outcomes

When planning for major financial decisions, it is imperative to anticipate unexpected outcomes and have contingency plans in place to address them effectively. While we may meticulously plan and analyze our choices, life is unpredictable, and unforeseen circumstances can arise that challenge our initial assumptions.

Developing contingency plans involves identifying potential risks and creating strategies to mitigate their impact. This proactive approach can help minimize the negative effects of unexpected events and ensure that your financial goals remain on track, even in the face of adversity.

One key aspect of developing contingency plans is to allocate resources for emergencies or unforeseen expenses. Setting aside a designated emergency fund can provide a financial safety net during challenging times and prevent you from derailing your long-term financial plans.

Another important component of contingency planning is to brainstorm various scenarios that could deviate from your original financial decision. By considering different possibilities and their potential consequences, you can better prepare for unexpected outcomes and make informed decisions when circumstances change.

It is also crucial to revisit and revise your contingency plans regularly. As your financial situation evolves and external factors shift, updating your strategies to reflect current realities is essential to maintaining financial stability and adaptability.

In conclusion, developing contingency plans for unexpected outcomes is a vital aspect of strategic financial planning. By proactively addressing potential risks, allocating resources for emergencies, considering various scenarios, and regularly revisiting your plans, you can enhance your resilience and preparedness in the face of uncertainty.

Reflecting on the Decision-Making Process and Learning from Past Experiences

Reflecting on the Decision-Making Process and Learning from Past Experiences requires a deep sense of introspection. Every major financial decision you make as a couple should be viewed as a learning opportunity. By looking back at the choices you've made, analyzing the outcomes, and understanding the lessons embedded in them, you can pave the way for greater financial wisdom in the future.

Take the time to review the decisions you've made together, both the successful ones and the ones that didn't turn out as expected. Look at the factors that influenced your choices, the information you had at the time, and the emotions that may have played a role in the decision-making process. By dissecting each decision with honesty and clarity, you can uncover valuable insights that will guide your future financial paths.

Learning from past experiences also involves acknowledging your mistakes and shortcomings. Be willing to confront any missteps or errors in judgment that may have led to undesirable outcomes. Instead of dwelling on the negative aspects, use these experiences as stepping stones for growth and improvement. Understand why certain decisions didn't work out and how you can avoid similar pitfalls in the future.

Moreover, celebrate your successes and achievements. Recognize the decisions that have brought you closer to your financial goals and acknowledge the positive impact they have had on your relationship. By appreciating your wins, you reinforce the good practices and strategies that have worked well for you.

Lastly, use the knowledge gained from reflecting on your decision-making process to refine your future strategies. Take heed of the lessons learned and apply them to upcoming financial decisions. By incorporating the wisdom gained from past experiences, you and your partner can navigate future challenges with greater confidence and foresight.

Dealing with Debt and Financial Challenges as a Team

Understanding the Impact of Debt on Your Relationship

Debt can be a weighty burden that affects not only your financial well-being but also the very fabric of your relationship. The stress and strain of debt can seep into all aspects of your life, casting a shadow on your happiness and harmony as a couple. It can create tension, arguments, and feelings of resentment if left unchecked. Debt has the power to strain communication, trust, and intimacy, making it crucial to address its impact on your relationship head-on. Understanding how debt affects your dynamic as a couple is the first step towards finding a way out of its grasp and moving forward together.

Assessing Your Current Financial Situation

Assessing Your Current Financial Situation:

Assessing your current financial situation is a crucial step in taking control of your debt and building a stronger financial foundation. It involves evaluating your income, expenses, assets, and liabilities to get a clear understanding of where you stand financially.

Begin by gathering all relevant financial documents, such as bank statements, credit card statements, loan statements, pay stubs, and any other income sources. Take stock of your monthly expenses, including fixed costs like rent or mortgage payments, utilities, and insurance, as well as variable expenses like groceries, dining out, entertainment, and other discretionary spending.

Next, list all your debts, including credit card balances, student loans, car loans, and any other outstanding debts. Note the interest rates, minimum monthly payments, and total balances for each debt. Understanding the full scope of your debt obligations is essential for developing a clear debt repayment strategy.

Compare your income to your expenses to determine your current cash flow situation. Are you consistently spending more than you earn? Are there areas where you can cut back on expenses to free up more money for debt repayment? Identifying potential areas for saving and reducing costs is key to improving your financial situation.

Finally, assess your assets, such as savings accounts, retirement funds, investments, and any other valuable possessions. Consider how these assets can be leveraged to help pay down debt or build a more secure financial future. By taking a comprehensive look at your financial picture, you can lay the groundwork for setting clear debt repayment goals and creating a plan to achieve them.

Setting Clear Debt Repayment Goals Together

Facing the reality of debt can be daunting, but setting clear debt repayment goals together is a crucial step towards financial freedom. It requires a deep dive into your current financial situation and a commitment to work collaboratively towards a common objective. By aligning your goals and priorities, you can create a roadmap to tackle your debts strategically and effectively.

Start by identifying all your existing debts, including credit card balances, loans, and any other financial obligations. Calculate the total amount owed, the interest rates, and minimum monthly payments for each debt. This comprehensive overview will provide you with a clear picture of the magnitude of your debt and serve as a foundation for setting realistic repayment goals.

Next, discuss your financial goals as a couple and prioritize debt repayment within your overarching financial plan. Define specific, measurable goals for paying off your debts, such as a target amount to repay within a certain timeframe. By establishing clear objectives, you can maintain focus and motivation throughout the debt repayment process.

Consider factors such as your income, expenses, and other financial commitments when determining how much you can allocate towards debt repayment each month. Strive to strike a balance between making substantial progress on repaying your debts and maintaining a sustainable budget that covers your essential expenses and savings goals.

To enhance accountability and transparency, create a written debt repayment plan that outlines your goals, timelines, and strategies. Break down your overall debt repayment goal into smaller milestones and track your progress regularly. Celebrate each milestone achieved as a couple, reinforcing your commitment to working together towards financial stability.

Communicate openly and honestly with each other about your financial situation, challenges, and progress towards debt repayment goals. Stay united in your efforts and provide mutual support and encouragement as you navigate the complexities of debt repayment. Remember that by facing this challenge together, you can strengthen your relationship and build a solid foundation for a secure financial future.

Exploring Debt Repayment Strategies and Options

Exploring Debt Repayment Strategies and Options:

When tackling debt as a couple, it is crucial to explore various strategies and options to effectively reduce and eliminate your financial burdens. One approach is the snowball method, where you focus on paying off your smallest debts first while making minimum payments on larger debts. This method can provide a sense of accomplishment and motivation as you see your smaller debts disappear.

Another strategy is the avalanche method, which involves prioritizing debts with the highest interest rates. By targeting these high-interest debts first, you can save money in the long run by reducing overall interest payments. This method may be more financially advantageous but can require patience and discipline.

Debt consolidation is an option that involves combining multiple debts into a single, more manageable loan with a lower interest rate. This can simplify your repayment process and potentially lower your monthly payments. However, it is important to carefully consider the terms and fees associated with debt consolidation before proceeding.

Negotiating with creditors is also a valuable strategy to explore. You may be able to work out a repayment plan or settlement that is more affordable and manageable for your financial situation. Communication is key in these negotiations, so be prepared to explain your circumstances honestly and provide any necessary documentation.

Seeking help from a financial advisor or credit counselor can provide valuable guidance and support in developing a debt repayment plan tailored to your specific needs. These professionals can offer expert advice on budgeting, debt management, and financial planning to help you achieve your goals.

Ultimately, the key to exploring debt repayment strategies and options as a couple is to approach the process with open communication, patience, and a shared commitment to achieving financial freedom. By working together and staying focused on your goals, you can overcome debt challenges and build a solid financial foundation for your future together.

Communicating Openly about Financial Challenges and Concerns

Effective communication is key to successfully navigating financial challenges as a couple. It is essential to create a safe and open space where both partners feel comfortable sharing their concerns and discussing their financial situation. Remember to listen actively and empathetically, without judgment or blame. Be honest and transparent about your individual struggles and worries regarding debt repayment. Set aside dedicated time to have regular check-ins and open discussions about your progress, setbacks, and goals. By openly communicating about your financial challenges and concerns, you can strengthen your relationship and work together towards a common solution.

Creating a Joint Plan to Tackle Debt as a Team

Debt can often feel like a heavy burden weighing down on both partners in a relationship. It's crucial to approach this challenge together with a united front. By creating a joint plan to tackle debt as a team, you can work towards a shared goal and strengthen your bond in the process. Start by laying out all the debts you both have, including amounts owed, interest rates, and minimum monthly payments. This clear overview will help you understand the scope of the debt and devise a strategy to address it.

Next, prioritize your debts based on interest rates or balances. Consider whether consolidating debts or negotiating with creditors could help lower interest rates or create more manageable repayment terms. Discuss your individual strengths and weaknesses when it comes to money management and debt repayment. By leveraging each other's skills and abilities, you can create a more effective debt repayment plan.

Set specific and achievable goals for paying off your debts. Decide on a timeline for when you aim to be debt-free and break down this goal into smaller milestones along the way. Regularly review your progress together and make adjustments to your plan as needed. Stay motivated by celebrating each milestone you reach, no matter how small.

Communication is key throughout this process. Keep each other informed about any changes in your financial situation and be transparent about your spending habits. By working together and supporting each other through the challenges of debt repayment, you can strengthen your relationship and build a solid foundation for a financially secure future.

Supporting Each Other Emotionally and Mentally Through Financial Difficulties

Financial challenges can place a significant strain on a relationship, often testing the emotional and mental fortitude of both partners. It is crucial to understand that navigating these difficult times as a team is essential for maintaining a strong and supportive bond.

During times of financial hardship, it is important to practice empathy and compassion towards each other. Recognize that both partners may be experiencing stress, anxiety, and frustration, and offering emotional support can help alleviate some of these shared burdens. Encourage open communication and create a safe space for expressing feelings and concerns without judgment.

Remember that financial difficulties are a temporary setback and not a reflection of your worth as individuals or as a couple. Stay committed to working together towards a common goal of overcoming these challenges, and remind each other of the strengths and qualities that brought you together in the first place.

Find ways to lift each other's spirits during tough times, whether it's through small gestures of kindness, words of encouragement, or simply being present and attentive to each other's needs. By strengthening your emotional connection and solidarity, you can weather the storm of financial difficulties with resilience and unity.

Seeking support from friends, family, or a therapist can also provide valuable outlets for processing emotions and seeking guidance during tough times. Remember that it's okay to ask for help when needed and that seeking professional assistance is a sign of strength, not weakness.

By supporting each other emotionally and mentally through financial difficulties, you can not only strengthen your relationship but also emerge stronger and more resilient as a team. Stay united, communicate openly, and lean on each other for strength and understanding during these challenging times.

Seeking Professional Help or Financial Counseling if Needed

Seeking professional help or financial counseling is a crucial step in addressing debt and financial challenges as a couple. When faced with overwhelming debt or financial stress, reaching out to a qualified financial advisor or counselor can provide valuable guidance and support.

Financial professionals have the knowledge and expertise to help you navigate complex financial situations and develop effective strategies for managing debt. They can offer objective advice and personalized solutions based on your unique financial circumstances.

By seeking professional help, you demonstrate a proactive approach to addressing your financial difficulties and seeking viable solutions. A financial counselor can help you understand the root causes of your financial challenges and work with you to create a realistic plan for debt repayment and financial stability.

Moreover, financial counseling can also help improve communication and decision-making within your relationship. It provides a neutral space for both partners to express their concerns, fears, and financial goals, fostering a deeper understanding and unity in tackling financial issues together.

Remember, seeking professional help is not a sign of weakness but a proactive step towards achieving financial well-being and stability. It is an investment in your future as a couple and a path towards building a stronger foundation for your relationship.

Monitoring Progress and Adjusting Strategies as Necessary

Monitoring progress is essential when dealing with debt and financial challenges as a team. Regularly tracking your debt repayment efforts allows you to stay on course towards your financial goals. By monitoring your progress, you can assess what strategies are working well and where adjustments may be needed.

Create a system to track your debt repayment progress, such as a spreadsheet or financial tracking tool. Record all payments made towards your debt, as well as any changes in your financial situation. This will give you a clear picture of how much debt you have paid off and how much remains.

Review your progress regularly as a couple and discuss any challenges or successes you have experienced. Use this time to reflect on your financial goals and make any necessary adjustments to your debt repayment plan. If you are not making the progress you had hoped for, brainstorm together to find new strategies to accelerate your debt repayment.

Celebrate small victories along the way to keep yourselves motivated. Acknowledge the progress you have made, no matter how small, and use it as a source of encouragement to continue working towards your larger financial goals. At the same time, be prepared to learn from any setbacks you may encounter. Identify the factors that led to the setback and use them as lessons to adjust your strategies moving forward.

By monitoring your progress and adjusting your strategies as necessary, you and your partner can stay focused and determined on your journey to becoming debt-free. Working together as a team and staying committed to your financial goals will ultimately lead you to a more secure and stable financial future.

Celebrating Victories and Learning from Setbacks as a Team

When celebrations arise from financial victories achieved through teamwork, it is important to acknowledge and appreciate the hard work and dedication that led to those successes. By recognizing these accomplishments together, you can strengthen your bond as a couple and further motivate each other in your financial journey.

It is equally crucial to learn from setbacks and challenges encountered along the way. These obstacles can serve as valuable lessons that help you navigate future financial decisions with more wisdom and resilience. Embrace setbacks as opportunities for growth and improvement, viewing them as stepping stones towards a stronger financial foundation.

Reflect on the setbacks experienced as a team, identifying the factors that contributed to the challenges faced. Use these insights to adjust your strategies and approaches moving forward, ensuring that you are better equipped to overcome similar obstacles in the future. By learning from setbacks and adapting your financial plan accordingly, you demonstrate your commitment to continuous improvement and financial success as a team.

Keep in mind that setbacks are a natural part of any financial journey, and they should not discourage you from pursuing your goals together. Instead, view them as opportunities to strengthen your partnership, enhance your problem-solving skills, and deepen your understanding of each other's financial values and priorities. Celebrate the victories achieved as a team, no matter how big or small, and use setbacks as valuable learning experiences that bring you closer together on your path to financial prosperity.

Strategies for Sharing Expenses Fairly

Understanding Individual Financial Situations

Understanding Individual Financial Situations

It is crucial to take the time to thoroughly understand your own financial situation before embarking on any shared financial journey with your partner. This involves a deep dive into your income, expenses, savings, investments, debts, and overall financial goals. By gaining a clear understanding of where you stand financially, you can better communicate your needs, preferences, and limitations to your partner.

Start by assessing your current income sources, including salaries, bonuses, side hustles, or any other sources of revenue. Understand the stability of your income streams and whether they fluctuate seasonally or remain consistent throughout the year. This will give you a sense of how much you can contribute to shared expenses and savings goals.

Next, analyze your expenses in detail. Consider fixed costs such as rent or mortgage payments, utilities, insurance, and loan repayments, as well as variable expenses like groceries, entertainment, and discretionary spending. Understanding where your money is going each month can help you identify areas where you can cut back to achieve your financial goals.

Take stock of your savings and investments, including retirement accounts, emergency funds, and any other assets you may have. Knowing your financial reserves and long-term savings goals will give you a sense of financial security and enable you to plan for the future with confidence.

Lastly, assess your debts and liabilities, such as credit card balances, student loans, or mortgages. Understanding the interest rates, repayment terms, and total outstanding amounts can help you prioritize debt repayment and avoid unnecessary financial strain.

By gaining a comprehensive understanding of your individual financial situation, you can approach shared finances with clarity, transparency, and a sense of responsibility. This foundational knowledge will set the stage for open communication, mutual goal setting, and effective financial planning as a couple.

Setting Clear Financial Expectations and Goals

Setting clear financial expectations and goals is crucial in ensuring a harmonious approach to managing expenses as a couple. It is essential to have open and honest conversations about your individual financial values, priorities, and long-term aspirations. By aligning your expectations and setting common goals, you lay a solid foundation for a successful financial partnership.

Take the time to discuss your short-term and long-term financial objectives. Consider your desired lifestyle, career aspirations, retirement plans, and any major purchases or investments you wish to make in the future. Understanding each other's financial aspirations will help in creating a shared vision for your financial future.

Clearly defining your financial expectations also involves discussing your attitudes towards spending, saving, and investing. Be transparent about your financial habits, including any potential areas of concern or disagreement. By addressing these differences early on, you can proactively find solutions and compromises that work for both partners.

Set realistic and achievable financial goals that reflect your combined values and priorities. Whether it's saving for a down payment on a house, funding a dream vacation, or investing in your children's education, having specific goals in place provides direction and motivation in your financial journey. Break down these goals into actionable steps and establish a timeline for achieving them.

Furthermore, consider the role of individual contributions to your shared financial responsibilities. Determine how each partner will contribute to joint expenses, savings, and investments based on your respective financial situations and capabilities. Establishing a fair and equitable contribution system ensures that both partners feel valued and respected in the financial decision-making process.

By setting clear financial expectations and goals as a couple, you pave the way for effective communication, collaboration, and financial success in your relationship. Clarity and alignment in your financial vision will guide your decisions and actions towards a secure and fulfilling future together.

Establishing a Fair Contribution System

When establishing a fair contribution system within a relationship, it is vital to consider each individual's financial situation and capabilities. This involves open communication and transparency regarding income, expenses, and financial goals. By setting clear expectations and understanding each other's perspectives, you can work together to create a system that is equitable and sustainable for both parties.

Differences on income level and expenses play a significant role in determining what constitutes a fair contribution from each partner. It is important to acknowledge any disparities in income and financial obligations, and to find a balance that considers these differences. This may involve a proportional contribution based on income percentages, or a shared responsibility for specific expenses based on individual capabilities.

Establishing a fair contribution system requires a delicate balance between equal partnership and understanding individual circumstances. It is essential to approach this process with empathy, respect, and a shared commitment to financial well-being. By working together to find a system that works for both parties, you can build a foundation of trust and mutual support in managing shared expenses.

Considering Income Disparities and Expenses

When considering income disparities and expenses in a relationship, it's essential to acknowledge and respect each other's financial situations. Some couples may have significantly different income levels due to various factors such as career choices, educational backgrounds, or personal circumstances. It is crucial to have open and honest discussions about these differences to understand each other's financial constraints and capabilities.

Before making any decisions regarding shared expenses, take the time to assess both partners' incomes, expenses, and financial obligations. Consider creating a detailed list of each person's monthly income, including salary, bonuses, investments, and any other sources of revenue. Similarly, compile a comprehensive list of expenses, including fixed costs such as rent, utilities, and loan payments, as well as variable expenses like groceries, entertainment, and personal expenditures.

Once you have a clear understanding of your financial situation as a couple, it's important to evaluate how best to allocate shared expenses. In cases where there is a significant income gap between partners, consider adjusting the contribution system to reflect each person's financial capacity. This may involve dividing expenses proportionally based on income percentages or finding alternative ways to balance financial obligations.

Additionally, when managing shared expenses, it's crucial to prioritize essential costs and allocate funds accordingly. By creating a joint budget that outlines necessary expenses and discretionary spending, you can ensure that both partners' financial needs are met while also working towards common financial goals. Remember to regularly review and adjust your budget as needed to accommodate changing financial circumstances.

Ultimately, navigating income disparities and expenses in a relationship requires empathy, understanding, and effective communication. By approaching financial discussions with sensitivity and respect for each other's perspectives, you can create a fair and equitable system that promotes financial harmony and stability in your partnership.

Budgeting for Shared Expenses

When budgeting for shared expenses as a couple, it is essential to approach the task with careful consideration and thoughtful planning. Shared expenses can encompass a wide range of items, including rent or mortgage payments, utilities, groceries, transportation costs, and entertainment expenses. To ensure that both partners feel comfortable and supported in their financial contributions, creating a clear and detailed budget is crucial.

When creating a budget for shared expenses, start by listing out all the necessary and discretionary expenses that you both incur on a regular basis. This could include fixed expenses like rent or mortgage payments, utilities, and insurance premiums, as well as variable expenses such as groceries, dining out, and entertainment.

Once you have a comprehensive list of shared expenses, it's important to allocate responsibility for each item based on both partners' income levels and financial capabilities. If there is a significant income disparity between partners, consider a proportional contribution system where each partner contributes a percentage of their income towards shared expenses rather than splitting costs evenly.

Additionally, it's important to build in a buffer for unexpected expenses or fluctuations in income. Consider setting aside a portion of your budget for a joint emergency fund to cover any unexpected costs that may arise.

Regularly reviewing and adjusting your shared expense budget is also crucial to ensure that it remains fair and equitable for both partners. Schedule monthly or quarterly budget meetings to discuss any changes in financial circumstances, expenses, or income levels, and make necessary adjustments to your budget as needed.

By proactively budgeting for shared expenses and working together to find a system that works for both partners, you can strengthen your financial partnership and build a solid foundation for long-term financial security and success.

Implementing a Joint Account or Expense Tracking System

When implementing a joint account or expense tracking system, it is crucial to establish clear guidelines and parameters to ensure transparency and accountability. This system can provide a shared platform for managing finances and tracking expenses, enabling both partners to have a comprehensive view of their financial situation.

First and foremost, consider the type of joint account that best suits your needs - whether it's a joint checking account for shared expenses or a joint savings account for specific financial goals. By consolidating funds in a joint account, both partners can contribute to and track expenses more efficiently.

Furthermore, setting up an expense tracking system can help monitor spending patterns, identify areas where adjustments can be made, and establish a solid financial foundation. This system can range from a simple spreadsheet to a more sophisticated budgeting tool, depending on your preferences and comfort level with financial management.

Regularly reviewing and updating the joint account or expense tracking system is essential to ensure that it remains effective and aligned with your financial goals. This practice can promote accountability, facilitate open communication about finances, and strengthen your financial partnership.

Incorporating a joint account or expense tracking system into your financial routine can streamline money management, foster collaboration in decision-making, and ultimately contribute to a healthier and more sustainable financial future.

Addressing Unequal Financial Contributions

When addressing unequal financial contributions in a relationship, it is essential to approach the situation with sensitivity and understanding. Financial disparities can arise for various reasons, such as differences in income, varying financial responsibilities, or unexpected financial challenges. It is crucial for both partners to acknowledge and discuss these discrepancies openly and honestly.

Communication is key when navigating unequal financial contributions. Both partners should be willing to have candid conversations about their individual financial situations, goals, and limitations. By sharing concerns and perspectives openly, couples can work towards finding a solution that feels fair and equitable to both parties.

One approach to addressing unequal financial contributions is to consider alternative ways to share expenses. This may involve a more flexible arrangement where each partner contributes based on their capacity or takes on specific financial responsibilities that align with their strengths and resources. By exploring creative solutions together, couples can find a balance that works for their unique circumstances.

It is also important to regularly evaluate and reassess financial contributions to ensure that the arrangement remains fair and sustainable. Circumstances may change over time, and it is essential for couples to revisit their financial agreement periodically to make any necessary adjustments. By staying proactive and communicative, couples can navigate unequal financial contributions with transparency and understanding.

Evaluating Financial Contributions Regularly

Regularly evaluating your financial contributions is a crucial aspect of maintaining fairness and transparency in your shared financial responsibilities. It ensures that both partners are actively engaged in monitoring and adjusting their financial commitments to suit their evolving circumstances. By regularly assessing your contributions, you can identify any discrepancies or areas where adjustments may be necessary to ensure a balanced financial partnership.

When evaluating financial contributions, it is essential to consider both quantitative and qualitative aspects. Quantitatively, assess the amount of money each partner contributes towards shared expenses, savings goals, and other financial obligations. Compare these contributions to ensure that they align with each partner's income and financial capacity.

Qualitative evaluation involves examining the non-monetary contributions that each partner brings to the table. Consider factors such as time spent managing finances, household responsibilities, and emotional support related to financial matters. These intangible contributions are equally valuable in a partnership and should be acknowledged and appreciated.

Regular financial evaluations provide an opportunity to have honest and open discussions about any concerns or challenges that may arise. It allows both partners to express their thoughts and feelings about their financial contributions and address any issues before they escalate. Communication is key in maintaining a healthy financial relationship, and regular evaluations foster transparency and understanding between partners.

In addition to assessing individual contributions, evaluating joint financial goals and progress is also essential. Review your financial goals, savings targets, and investment strategies regularly to ensure that you are on track to achieve them together. Adjust your contributions and financial plans as needed to stay aligned with your shared objectives and priorities.

By implementing regular evaluations of your financial contributions, you can strengthen your financial partnership and ensure that both partners feel valued and respected in their financial roles. It promotes accountability, trust, and collaboration in managing your finances as a team.

Communicating Openly About Financial Challenges

Effective communication is key when it comes to addressing financial challenges within a relationship. It is essential to create a safe and open space where both partners feel comfortable discussing their concerns and sharing their thoughts. Honest and transparent conversations about money issues can help strengthen trust and understanding between partners.

When faced with financial challenges, it is important to approach the situation with empathy and respect towards each other's perspectives. Listen actively to your partner's concerns and avoid placing blame or judgment. Instead, focus on finding solutions together as a team.

Discussing financial challenges openly also allows both partners to brainstorm potential ways to overcome obstacles and work towards a common goal. By sharing responsibilities and working together towards a solution, you can build a stronger foundation for your financial future.

It is also crucial to maintain regular communication about any changes in financial circumstances or unexpected expenses that may arise. By keeping each other informed, you can avoid misunderstandings and proactively address any potential issues before they escalate.

Remember that seeking external support or professional advice is always an option if you find yourselves struggling to navigate financial challenges on your own. A financial advisor or counselor can provide valuable insights and guidance to help you make informed decisions and develop a solid financial plan.

Overall, open and honest communication about financial challenges is essential for cultivating a healthy and sustainable relationship built on trust, understanding, and mutual support.

Seeking Professional Advice if Needed

Seeking Professional Advice if Needed

When facing complex financial challenges that seem overwhelming or beyond your expertise, it may be beneficial to seek professional advice. Financial advisors, accountants, or other specialists can provide valuable insights and guidance to help you navigate difficult financial situations.

Professional advice can offer a fresh perspective on your financial circumstances and help you develop effective strategies to address your challenges. These experts have the knowledge and experience to analyze your situation objectively and offer tailored solutions that align with your goals.

Working with a financial professional can also help you make well-informed decisions that may have a lasting impact on your financial well-being. Whether you need help with investment planning, debt management, tax optimization, or estate planning, seeking professional advice can provide you with the expertise and support you need to make sound financial choices.

Remember that seeking professional advice is not a sign of weakness but a smart and proactive approach to managing your finances. By collaborating with experts in the field, you can gain valuable insights, access specialized knowledge, and enhance your financial literacy to make informed decisions that align with your long-term financial goals.

Strategies for Sharing Expenses Fairly

Setting the Foundation of Trust

Setting the Foundation of Trust

Establishing open and honest communication about financial matters is essential for fostering trust within a relationship. Money plays a significant role in our lives and can often be a sensitive topic. By creating a safe space for discussing money without judgment, partners can build a strong foundation of trust and understanding.

Transparency is key when it comes to sharing financial information. Being open about individual incomes, expenses, and financial goals helps create clarity and alignment in the relationship. Full disclosure builds trust and allows partners to make informed decisions together.

When it comes to joint decision making, both partners should have a say in financial matters. Considering each other's perspectives and working towards consensus on major money-related choices strengthens the bond and shows mutual respect.

Being accountable and responsible for financial commitments is crucial. By holding each other accountable and taking ownership of individual contributions to the relationship's financial health, partners demonstrate reliability and commitment to each other.

Respecting financial boundaries and priorities is another aspect of building trust. Understanding and honoring differences in money management styles shows appreciation for each other's values and helps avoid conflicts related to finances.

Regular financial check-ins help partners stay on track with their financial goals. Setting aside time to review finances and discuss any concerns ensures that both partners are aligned and committed to their shared financial future.

Navigating financial challenges as a team is a testament to the strength of the relationship. By facing unexpected expenses or setbacks together, partners can demonstrate solidarity and support for each other during tough times.

Building trust through actions is essential. Following through on financial promises, demonstrating reliability, and showing responsibility in money matters all contribute to a strong foundation of trust within the relationship.

Seeking professional guidance when needed can also strengthen the relationship. Considering financial counseling or therapy for addressing deeper money-related issues and consulting with a financial advisor or planner for long-term planning shows a commitment to the relationship's financial well-being.

Finally, reaffirming trust and solidarity through celebrating financial milestones and achievements together can help partners recognize and appreciate the journey they have taken to build a foundation of trust in their relationship.

Sharing Financial Information

Sharing financial information is a crucial aspect of building trust and transparency in a relationship. It involves being open and honest about your individual financial situations, including income, expenses, savings, and debts. By sharing this information with your partner, you are creating a foundation of trust that enables both of you to make informed decisions together.

When you share your financial information with your partner, you are inviting them into your financial world and giving them a deeper understanding of your financial values, beliefs, and goals. This level of transparency fosters a sense of closeness and unity in the relationship, as you are both actively involved in each other's financial well-being.

Being honest about your financial situation also allows for better collaboration when it comes to making joint financial decisions. It eliminates any surprises or misunderstandings that may arise if one partner is unaware of the other's financial details. By sharing this information, you are creating a level playing field where both partners have an equal say in financial matters.

Moreover, sharing financial information can help you both identify areas where you can work together to improve your financial health. It allows you to see the big picture of your combined finances and work towards common financial goals. By openly discussing your financial information, you can uncover any potential issues or obstacles and address them as a team.

Overall, sharing financial information is an essential step towards building trust, unity, and collaboration in your relationship. It sets the stage for open communication, joint decision-making, and a strong foundation for navigating your financial journey together.

Joint Decision Making

Joint Decision Making involves coming together as a team to navigate the complexities of financial choices. It requires a deep level of communication, respect, and collaboration to ensure that both partners feel heard and valued. When making decisions about money, it is crucial to consider each other's perspectives and find common ground. By working together, couples can create a sense of shared responsibility and investment in their financial future. It's essential to approach financial decision-making with a spirit of cooperation and understanding, recognizing that both partners bring unique insights and experiences to the table. By embracing joint decision-making, couples can strengthen their bond and build a solid foundation for financial harmony.

Accountability and Responsibility

Accountability and Responsibility

Holding each other accountable for our financial commitments is essential for maintaining trust and harmony in our relationship. When we take ownership of our individual contributions to our financial well-being, we show respect and dedication to this partnership. It is not enough to merely agree on financial goals; we must actively work towards them with honesty and integrity.

Being accountable means following through on the promises we make regarding money matters. Whether it's sticking to our budget, saving diligently, or avoiding unnecessary expenses, our actions must align with our shared financial priorities. By holding ourselves accountable, we show that we are reliable and trustworthy partners in this journey towards financial stability.

Responsibility goes hand in hand with accountability. We each have a role to play in managing our finances and ensuring our financial health. This includes being honest about our income, expenses, and financial decisions, as well as being proactive in addressing any challenges that may arise. Taking responsibility for our financial well-being shows that we are committed to our shared goals and are willing to put in the effort required to achieve them.

When we are accountable and responsible for our financial actions, we demonstrate our commitment to the relationship and our respect for each other's financial boundaries. By working together towards a common goal and facing our financial challenges as a united front, we strengthen the foundation of trust that is vital for a healthy and successful partnership.

Financial Boundaries and Respect

Establishing and respecting financial boundaries is crucial in maintaining a healthy and balanced relationship. Each partner brings their own unique perspective and values when it comes to money management. It is essential to recognize and honor these differences, creating a space where both individuals feel heard and understood.

Respect plays a key role in navigating financial boundaries. It involves acknowledging each other's financial goals, priorities, and limitations without judgment or criticism. By respecting each other's views on money matters, you can cultivate a sense of trust and mutual understanding within the relationship.

Setting clear boundaries around finances helps define each partner's responsibilities and expectations. This clarity can prevent misunderstandings or conflicts down the line. Whether it involves individual spending habits, saving goals, or investment decisions, having open discussions about these boundaries can foster a sense of security and stability in the relationship.

Respecting financial boundaries also means being mindful of each other's comfort levels when it comes to money-related topics. Some individuals may be more private about their finances, while others may be more open to sharing details. By respecting these differences, you can create a safe and supportive environment for discussing money matters.

Communication is key in establishing and maintaining financial boundaries. Regular conversations about financial values, goals, and expectations can help reinforce mutual respect and understanding. By actively listening to each other's perspectives and being open to compromise, you can strengthen your financial partnership and lay the foundation for a successful and harmonious relationship.

Regular Financial Check-Ins

Regular Financial Check-Ins

Establishing a routine for regular financial check-ins is crucial for maintaining transparency and trust in your relationship. These check-ins provide an opportunity to review your financial progress, address any concerns, and ensure you are both on track towards your shared goals.

Schedule dedicated time each month to sit down and discuss your finances. Use this time to go over your income, expenses, savings, and investments. Take note of any changes or unexpected expenses that may have occurred since your last check-in.

During these sessions, encourage open and honest communication about money matters. Listen actively to each other's financial concerns and goals. Discuss any discrepancies or areas where you can improve your financial management as a couple.

Set specific agendas for your financial discussions to ensure you cover all relevant topics. This could include reviewing your budget, tracking your spending patterns, evaluating your progress towards savings goals, and discussing any upcoming financial decisions or challenges.

Use your financial check-ins as a way to celebrate your achievements and milestones. Recognize the progress you've made together and acknowledge the hard work and dedication you've both put into managing your finances as a team.

Regular financial check-ins not only help you stay organized but also strengthen your bond as a couple. By committing to these meetings, you demonstrate your willingness to work together towards a secure financial future and reinforce the trust and respect in your relationship.

Handling Financial Challenges as a Team

During your financial journey as a couple, there will undoubtedly be challenges that test your ability to work together as a team. These challenges may come in the form of unexpected expenses, fluctuations in income, or disagreements about financial priorities. It is during these times that your ability to communicate effectively, show empathy, and work towards a common solution will be crucial.

Handling financial challenges as a team requires a united front and a willingness to confront the issue head-on. Avoiding difficult conversations about money can lead to resentment and further strain on your relationship. Instead, approach these challenges with a sense of unity and a shared commitment to finding a solution together.

When faced with financial difficulties, take the time to assess the situation calmly and rationally. Identify the root cause of the problem and consider potential solutions that align with your shared financial goals. Communicate openly about your concerns, fears, and hopes regarding the situation, and listen actively to your partner's perspective as well.

It is essential to approach financial challenges from a problem-solving mindset rather than placing blame or judgment on each other. Remember that you are a team, and working together to overcome obstacles will strengthen your bond and build trust in your relationship.

Consider seeking outside support if needed, whether it be from a financial advisor, counselor, or trusted mentor. Professional guidance can provide you with additional tools and insights to navigate difficult financial situations effectively.

By facing financial challenges as a team, you demonstrate your commitment to each other and your shared future. Embrace these challenges as opportunities for growth, learning, and strengthening your relationship through resilience and unity.

Building Trust Through Actions

Building Trust Through Actions

Trust is the cornerstone of a strong and lasting relationship, especially when it comes to managing finances together. It is through consistent actions and behaviors that trust is built and maintained in the realm of money matters.

One key way to build trust is by following through on financial promises and commitments. Whether it's sticking to a budget, saving for a shared goal, or paying bills on time, keeping your word reinforces reliability and responsibility in your partner's eyes.

Demonstrating openness and honesty in financial matters is another crucial element in building trust. Being transparent about your income, expenses, and financial decisions fosters a sense of trust and unity in your relationship. It shows that you value your partner's input and respect their right to know where the money is going.

Taking ownership of your financial contributions and responsibilities also plays a significant role in building trust. When each partner takes responsibility for their share of the financial obligations and actively participates in the money management process, it creates a sense of fairness, equity, and trust in the relationship.

Furthermore, showing empathy and understanding towards your partner's money-related concerns helps strengthen the bond of trust between you. By listening attentively, offering support, and being sensitive to each other's financial fears or anxieties, you demonstrate that you are a reliable and caring partner in navigating the ups and downs of money matters together.

Lastly, celebrating financial milestones and achievements as a team reinforces trust and solidarity in your relationship. Whether it's reaching a savings goal, paying off a debt, or making a smart investment decision, taking the time to acknowledge and celebrate these victories together highlights your shared commitment, dedication, and trust in each other's financial capabilities.

In essence, building trust through actions is a continuous process that requires consistent effort, communication, and respect in managing your finances together. By prioritizing trust in your financial relationship, you lay a strong foundation for a healthy and enduring partnership built on mutual respect, transparency, and shared financial goals.

Seeking Professional Guidance

Seeking Professional Guidance

Navigating the complexities of finances within a relationship can often be challenging. In times of uncertainty or conflict regarding money matters, seeking the assistance of a professional can provide valuable insight and guidance. Financial counselors or therapists specialize in helping couples address deep-rooted money-related issues, offering a neutral perspective to facilitate open and productive conversations.

Additionally, enlisting the expertise of a financial advisor or planner can help create a roadmap for long-term financial stability and success. These professionals can offer customized solutions tailored to your specific financial goals and circumstances, providing valuable strategies for budgeting, saving, investing, and planning for the future.

By seeking professional guidance, couples can gain valuable tools and resources to navigate financial challenges, enhance communication, and strengthen their financial foundation. Embracing the support and expertise of professionals can foster a deeper understanding of each other's financial values and goals, ultimately leading to a more aligned and harmonious approach to money management.

Reaffirming Trust and Solidarity

Celebrating financial milestones and achievements together is a crucial aspect of reaffirming trust and solidarity in a relationship. These moments serve as markers of progress and success, highlighting the shared effort and dedication that both partners have put into their financial journey. Whether it's reaching a savings goal, paying off a significant debt, or achieving a long-held financial dream, each milestone is an opportunity to celebrate and reflect on the strength of your partnership.

Acknowledging and celebrating these accomplishments not only fosters a sense of pride and satisfaction but also reinforces the bond between partners. It validates the shared vision and commitment to financial well-being, reminding you both of the power of working together towards a common goal. By taking the time to recognize and honor these achievements, you not only reaffirm trust and solidarity but also create lasting memories that strengthen your relationship.

In the midst of the daily challenges and responsibilities of managing finances, it's essential to pause and commemorate the milestones along the way. These celebrations can take many forms, from a simple toast or dinner together to a special outing or trip to mark the occasion. The key is to find meaningful ways to honor the hard work and dedication that have brought you to this point and to reaffirm your unity in facing future financial goals together.

By celebrating your financial milestones together, you not only create moments of joy and connection but also lay a foundation for continued trust and solidarity in your relationship. It's a reminder of the victories you've achieved as a team and an affirmation of the strength and resilience you possess as partners in navigating the ups and downs of your financial journey. So take the time to acknowledge and celebrate your milestones, for they are not just markers of success but also tokens of the trust and solidarity that bind you together.

Celebrating Financial Milestones

Recognizing Achievements: Reflecting on the journey and acknowledging the milestones reached

Reflecting on the journey thus far, it is crucial to pause and acknowledge the milestones that have been achieved along the way. Each step taken, each goal reached, each challenge overcome, represents a significant achievement in your financial journey. It is important to take a moment to celebrate these accomplishments, no matter how big or small they may seem.

By recognizing these achievements, you affirm your progress and hard work. It serves as a reminder of your dedication and commitment to improving your financial well-being. Reflecting on the milestones reached allows you to see how far you have come and motivates you to continue moving forward. It instills a sense of pride and accomplishment, boosting your confidence in your ability to achieve future goals.

Acknowledging these milestones is not just about patting yourself on the back; it is about understanding the value of the effort you have put in. It is about recognizing the sacrifices made, the obstacles overcome, and the lessons learned along the way. Each achievement represents a moment of growth and progress, a testament to your resilience and determination in pursuing financial success.

In the midst of striving towards bigger goals, it can be easy to overlook the significance of the smaller victories. However, it is these incremental successes that pave the way for larger achievements. By taking the time to reflect on and acknowledge the milestones reached, you reaffirm your commitment to your financial journey and set a positive tone for the challenges that lie ahead.

So, take a moment to celebrate your achievements, no matter how humble they may seem. Recognize the progress you have made, the hurdles you have overcome, and the growth you have experienced. Embrace the journey and acknowledge the milestones reached with a sense of gratitude and appreciation for the hard work and dedication that have brought you this far.

Cultivating Gratitude: Embracing the abundance that comes with achieving financial goals and expressing thankfulness for progress made

Gratitude is a powerful emotion that allows us to recognize and appreciate the abundance in our lives. When it comes to achieving financial milestones, cultivating gratitude can have a profound impact on our mindset and overall well-being. By taking the time to reflect on the progress we have made and expressing thankfulness for the steps we have taken, we not only acknowledge our achievements but also set the stage for continued success.

In the journey towards financial growth, gratitude serves as a guiding light that illuminates the path ahead. It reminds us of the hard work, dedication, and sacrifices that have contributed to our accomplishments. By embracing gratitude, we shift our focus from what we lack to what we have achieved, instilling a sense of fulfillment and contentment in our financial journey.

Expressing gratitude for our financial milestones is more than just a gesture of appreciation; it is a practice that fuels our motivation and determination. When we take the time to acknowledge the progress we have made, we reinforce our belief in our capabilities and resilience. Gratitude acts as a catalyst for further success, inspiring us to set new goals and strive towards even greater achievements.

As we navigate the complexities of financial planning and goal-setting, cultivating gratitude reminds us of the value of our journey.

It encourages us to celebrate not only the end results but also the small victories along the way. By embracing gratitude, we create a positive and optimistic outlook that propels us forward towards new opportunities and challenges.

In the realm of personal finance, gratitude is a cornerstone of success. It reminds us of the blessings we have received, the lessons we have learned, and the growth we have experienced. By embracing gratitude in our financial journey, we create a mindset of abundance and possibility, paving the way for continued growth, prosperity, and fulfillment.

Setting New Goals: Planning for the future by establishing new financial objectives to strive towards

As we reflect on the achievements we have made in our financial journey, it is crucial to turn our attention towards setting new goals. Establishing clear objectives for the future not only propels us forward but also ensures that we continue to grow and evolve financially. Setting new goals allows us to challenge ourselves, push our boundaries, and work towards a brighter and more prosperous future.

When it comes to financial goal-setting, it is essential to be specific, measurable, achievable, relevant, and time-bound. By defining our objectives with these SMART criteria in mind, we can create a roadmap that leads us towards success. Whether our goals involve saving for a major purchase, investing for retirement, or paying off debt, each goal should be carefully thought out and aligned with our long-term financial vision.

Moreover, setting new goals presents us with an opportunity to dream big and aim high. It encourages us to think beyond our current circumstances and envision a future filled with financial security and abundance. By daring to set ambitious goals, we challenge ourselves to reach new heights and surpass our own expectations.

As we embark on this journey of setting new financial goals, it is important to involve our partner or team in the process. By sharing our aspirations and collaborating on the goals we want to achieve, we not only strengthen our relationship but also increase our chances of success. Working together towards common financial objectives fosters a sense of unity and solidarity, reinforcing the idea that we are a team in pursuit of a shared vision.

In conclusion, setting new goals is an essential part of our financial growth and development. By planning for the future and establishing new objectives to strive towards, we set ourselves on a path towards continued success and fulfillment. Let us embrace this opportunity to dream, plan, and work diligently towards a future that is filled with financial prosperity and abundance.

Sharing Success: Celebrating as a couple or team and reinforcing the importance of teamwork in achieving financial milestones

Celebrating financial milestones as a couple or team is a way to not only acknowledge achievements but also to strengthen the bond and unity in pursuing shared goals. When you reach a significant milestone together, it's crucial to take the time to celebrate and acknowledge the hard work and dedication you both have put into your financial journey.

By sharing the success with your partner or team, you reinforce the importance of collaboration and support in achieving financial milestones. Celebrating together creates a sense of camaraderie and unity that can motivate and encourage each other to continue working towards future goals.

Whether it's a small victory or a major milestone, taking the time to celebrate the achievement as a couple or team can deepen your connection and build a sense of shared accomplishment. It also serves as a reminder of the power of teamwork and the value of working together towards a common purpose.

Through celebrating together, you not only honor the efforts you've invested in reaching your financial goals but also create lasting memories that can strengthen your relationship and inspire continued teamwork in your financial journey.

Rewarding Yourself: Treating yourself in a meaningful way to commemorate reaching a significant financial milestone

Recognize the dedication and effort you've put into achieving your financial milestone. Treat yourself to something special that aligns with your values and brings you joy. This reward serves as a tangible reminder of your hard work and commitment to your financial goals. It acts as a symbol of your progress and success, motivating you to continue on your journey towards financial freedom. Choose a reward that is meaningful to you, whether it's a small indulgence or a larger purchase you've been saving for. By acknowledging your accomplishments and rewarding yourself, you reinforce the positive habits and behaviors that have led to your success. Remember, celebrating yourself is an important part of staying motivated and staying on track with your financial goals.

Inspiring Others: Sharing your success story to motivate and inspire others on their financial journey

Sharing your success story can have a profound impact on those around you who may be on their own financial journey. By recounting your achievements and the steps you took to reach a significant milestone, you have the power to inspire and motivate others to pursue their own financial goals with determination and purpose.

When sharing your success story, authenticity is key. Be honest about the challenges you faced, the sacrifices you made, and the strategies that proved successful. By being transparent about your experiences, you can provide valuable insights and lessons that others can apply to their own financial situation.

Your success story can serve as a beacon of hope for those who may be feeling discouraged or overwhelmed by their financial struggles. By showcasing what is possible through hard work, perseverance, and smart financial decisions, you can ignite a sense of possibility and belief in others that they too can achieve financial success.

As you share your journey, be sure to highlight the importance of setting clear goals, creating a solid plan, and staying committed to your financial objectives. Emphasize the value of persistence and resilience in the face of challenges, and encourage others to stay focused on their long-term financial vision.

By sharing your success story, you have the opportunity to create a ripple effect of inspiration and empowerment in the lives of others. Your experiences and accomplishments can spark motivation and drive in those who may be striving to improve their financial well-being, ultimately helping them to realize their own potential and achieve their goals.

Maintaining Momentum: Leveraging the motivation from reaching a milestone to continue making progress towards larger financial goals

Leveraging the motivation from reaching a milestone is crucial in ensuring continued progress towards larger financial goals. It's easy to become complacent or satisfied after achieving a significant milestone, but maintaining momentum is key to sustaining long-term financial success.

Use the sense of accomplishment from reaching one milestone as fuel to propel you towards the next. Reflect on the hard work, discipline, and dedication that got you to this point, and let it inspire you to keep pushing forward. Remember that financial success is a journey, not a destination, and each milestone reached is a stepping stone towards greater financial freedom.

Stay focused on your objectives and regularly revisit your financial goals to remind yourself of what you are working towards. By setting new targets and constantly challenging yourself, you can harness the momentum from past achievements to drive you towards even bigger accomplishments.

Celebrate your victories but also remain humble and grounded, recognizing that there is always more to learn and achieve. Keep building on your successes, learning from your experiences, and adapting your financial strategies as needed. By staying motivated and driven, you can continue making steady progress towards your ultimate financial aspirations.

Reflecting on Lessons Learned: Analyzing the strategies and decisions that led to success and identifying key takeaways for future financial endeavors

Reflecting on the lessons learned from past financial milestones is crucial in guiding our future endeavors. By analyzing the strategies and decisions that led to success, we gain valuable insights that can shape our approach to larger financial goals. Looking back allows us to pinpoint what worked well and what could be improved upon, enabling us to make informed choices moving forward. It is an opportunity to assess our strengths and weaknesses, identify patterns in our financial behavior, and refine our strategies for sustainable success. Through this reflection, we can uncover valuable lessons that can serve as the foundation for a solid plan for ongoing financial growth and prosperity.

Planning for the Future: Incorporating the lessons learned from past milestones into a solid plan for ongoing financial success

As we look towards the future, it is crucial to incorporate the valuable lessons learned from past financial milestones into a strategic plan for ongoing success. Reflecting on our previous achievements allows us to pinpoint the strategies and decisions that have propelled us forward, as well as recognize areas where improvement is needed. By taking stock of what has worked well and what could be refined, we can establish a solid foundation for future financial endeavors.

Each milestone reached is a testament to our dedication and hard work, but it also serves as a roadmap for what lies ahead. By carefully evaluating the successes and setbacks of our financial journey, we gain invaluable insights that can guide us in setting new goals and making informed decisions moving forward. This reflection process is not just about celebrating past accomplishments but about leveraging them to create a clear, actionable plan for our financial future.

Incorporating the lessons learned from past milestones into our future financial strategy is about growth and evolution. It involves adapting to changing circumstances, learning from past experiences, and being willing to adjust our approach when necessary. By combining our newfound knowledge with a forward-thinking mindset, we can navigate the complexities of financial planning with confidence and precision.

As we plan for the future, let us remember that each milestone achieved is a stepping stone towards greater financial freedom. It is through the integration of past lessons into our present strategy that we pave the way for continued growth and success. By embracing the wisdom gained from our financial journey thus far, we can lay the groundwork for a prosperous and secure future.

Embracing Growth and Progress: Emphasizing personal and financial growth as an ongoing process and celebrating each milestone as a stepping stone towards greater financial freedom

As we continue on our financial journey, it is crucial to embrace growth and progress as integral parts of our ongoing process. Personal and financial development go hand in hand, with each milestone serving as a stepping stone towards greater financial freedom.

Every success and setback is an opportunity for learning and growth. By reflecting on our past achievements and challenges, we can gain valuable insights that will inform our future financial decisions. It is essential to incorporate these lessons learned into a solid plan for ongoing financial success.

Emphasizing the importance of personal growth allows us to develop a mindset geared towards continuous improvement. By setting new goals and pushing ourselves beyond our comfort zones, we can expand our financial horizons and reach new heights of success.

Celebrating each milestone, no matter how small, reinforces our progress and motivates us to keep moving forward. It is important to acknowledge the hard work and dedication that have brought us to where we are today, and to use that momentum to propel us towards our next financial objective.

Remember that growth and progress are not linear – there will be ups and downs along the way. The key is to stay focused on the bigger picture and remain committed to our long-term financial goals. By embracing the journey and recognizing that every step forward is a victory, we can cultivate a mindset of resilience and determination that will carry us through any challenges that come our way.

In essence, personal and financial growth are ongoing processes that require dedication, perseverance, and a willingness to adapt. By celebrating each milestone as a testament to our progress and a pathway to greater financial freedom, we can continue to evolve and thrive on our journey towards financial success.

The Power of Financial Freedom

Introduction to Financial Independence

Financial independence is a pinnacle many strive to reach—a state where one's financial resources are robust enough to support the desired lifestyle without the need for active employment. It signifies freedom from financial constraints and the ability to make choices based on personal values rather than financial obligations.

Achieving financial independence requires discipline, strategic planning, and a long-term mindset. It is not merely about accumulating wealth but also about developing sustainable financial habits that align with your goals and values. By actively working towards financial freedom, you are investing in your present and future self, empowering yourself to live life on your own terms.

The journey to financial independence goes beyond just accumulating money; it encompasses a holistic approach to managing resources, cultivating a healthy relationship with money, and embracing a mindset of abundance. It involves setting clear financial goals, creating a roadmap to achieve them, and remaining committed to the path even in the face of challenges.

Financial independence transcends monetary wealth; it is about gaining autonomy over your financial decisions, reducing stress related to money, and opening up opportunities for personal growth and fulfillment. It offers the freedom to pursue passions, invest in self-improvement, and contribute to causes that resonate with your values.

As you embark on the quest for financial independence, remember that it is a journey that requires patience, persistence, and continuous learning. Embrace the process, celebrate small victories along the way, and stay focused on the bigger picture of realizing your financial aspirations. Through dedication and mindful financial choices, you can navigate towards a future of abundance and security.

The Connection Between Financial Freedom and Personal Growth

Financial independence is not merely about accumulating wealth; it is a transformative journey that goes hand in hand with personal growth. The connection between financial freedom and personal development runs deep, as the pursuit of financial stability forces us to confront our beliefs, habits, and attitudes towards money. It challenges us to break free from self-imposed limitations and step into a mindset of abundance and empowerment.

Achieving financial freedom requires a shift in perspective—a willingness to reassess our relationship with money and make conscious decisions that align with our values and goals. It compels us to confront our fears, insecurities, and limiting beliefs about wealth and success. In doing so, we cultivate resilience, perseverance, and a sense of self-worth that transcends monetary measures.

As we strive towards financial independence, we are propelled to embrace change, take calculated risks, and challenge ourselves to grow beyond our comfort zones. The journey towards financial freedom is not just about accumulating wealth; it is about discovering our true potential, unlocking our innate creativity, and fostering a sense of empowerment that extends far beyond our financial circumstances.

In essence, the pursuit of financial freedom is a journey of self-discovery and personal transformation. It challenges us to redefine our priorities, set meaningful goals, and cultivate a mindset of abundance and possibility. By embarking on this journey, we open ourselves up to new opportunities, experiences, and perspectives that enrich our lives and propel us towards a future of limitless potential.

Breaking Free from Financial Constraints

Financial constraints can weigh heavily on our lives, restricting our choices and limiting our potential. Breaking free from these constraints requires a shift in mindset and a commitment to taking control of our financial well-being. It starts with facing our current financial situation head-on, understanding the root causes of our constraints, and making a plan to overcome them.

To break free from financial constraints, it is essential to prioritize financial stability and set clear financial goals. This involves creating a realistic budget, tracking expenses, and identifying areas where we can cut back on spending. By being mindful of our financial habits and making intentional choices with our money, we can start to regain control of our finances.

Another crucial aspect of breaking free from financial constraints is addressing any debt that may be holding us back. Developing a strategy to pay off debt systematically, whether through a debt snowball or avalanche method, can help us eliminate this burden and free up resources for building wealth and financial security.

It is also important to explore opportunities for increasing our income, whether through career advancement, side hustles, or investments. By actively seeking ways to boost our income, we can accelerate our journey towards financial freedom and break free from the constraints that have been holding us back.

Breaking free from financial constraints is a process that requires patience, diligence, and a willingness to make tough choices. By taking proactive steps to improve our financial situation, we can pave the way for a future of greater financial independence and security.

Building Wealth for Long-Term Security

Building wealth for long-term security requires a disciplined and strategic approach. It is not just about accumulating money but about creating a solid financial foundation that will support you through all stages of life. By implementing sound investment strategies and smart financial decisions, you can pave the way towards a secure and prosperous future.

Investing in assets that have the potential for long-term growth is essential for building wealth. Diversifying your investment portfolio across different asset classes can help spread risk and maximize returns. Whether it's stocks, bonds, real estate, or other investment vehicles, choose wisely based on your financial goals and risk tolerance.

In addition to investing, saving diligently is crucial for long-term financial security. Establishing an emergency fund to cover unexpected expenses and setting aside money for retirement are key components of a sustainable financial plan. By consistently saving a portion of your income and prioritizing financial goals, you can build wealth over time.

It's also important to regularly review and adjust your financial plan as needed. Life circumstances may change, and market conditions fluctuate, so staying informed and adaptive is essential. Seeking guidance from financial advisors or experts can provide valuable insights and help you make informed decisions about your financial future.

Building wealth is not a sprint but a marathon. It requires patience, discipline, and a long-term perspective. By staying focused on your financial goals, making smart choices, and being proactive in managing your finances, you can create a secure financial future for yourself and your loved ones.

Creating a Sustainable Financial Plan

Creating a sustainable financial plan involves carefully evaluating your current financial situation and setting realistic goals for the future. Begin by assessing your income, expenses, debts, and savings to get a clear picture of where you stand. From there, identify areas where you can cut back on unnecessary spending and allocate more towards savings and investments. It's essential to prioritize building an emergency fund to cover unexpected expenses and establish a solid financial foundation. Develop a budget that aligns with your financial goals and allows for both short-term needs and long-term aspirations. Consider working with a financial advisor to create a comprehensive plan that addresses retirement savings, investment strategies, and risk management. Regularly review and adjust your financial plan as needed to ensure you stay on track towards financial security and independence. By taking a proactive and strategic approach to managing your finances, you can create a sustainable plan that will support your long-term financial well-being.

Embracing a Mindful Approach to Money

Money is more than just a tool for transactions; it holds the power to shape our lives in profound ways. Our approach to money influences not only our financial well-being but also our overall sense of contentment and security. Embracing a mindful approach to money involves cultivating a deep awareness of our financial habits and beliefs. By practicing conscious spending and making intentional financial decisions, we can transform our relationship with money and pave the way for greater financial freedom.

Mindful spending goes beyond simply tracking expenses; it requires us to pause and reflect on the true value of our purchases. By considering the long-term impact of our financial choices, we can prioritize spending on things that align with our values and goals. This intentional approach helps us avoid impulsive purchases and instead focus on investments that contribute to our overall well-being.

In addition to mindful spending, cultivating a positive mindset towards money is essential for financial success. By viewing money as a tool for growth and empowerment, we can shift our perspective from scarcity to abundance. This mindset shift not only encourages proactive financial planning but also fosters a sense of gratitude for the resources we have.

Practicing mindfulness in our financial decisions also involves being present in the moment and fully engaging with our financial responsibilities. This includes regularly reviewing our financial goals, tracking our progress, and adjusting our plans as needed. By staying actively involved in our financial journey, we can make informed decisions that support our long-term financial well-being.

Ultimately, embracing a mindful approach to money is about bringing awareness and intentionality to our financial choices. By cultivating a deeper understanding of our relationship with money and adopting healthy financial habits, we can pave the way for financial freedom and abundance.

The Impact of Financial Freedom on Relationships

Financial freedom has a profound impact on relationships. When individuals are financially secure and responsible, it can positively influence their interactions with others. Money can often be a source of tension and conflicts in relationships, but achieving financial independence can help alleviate some of these stressors.

Couples who are both committed to financial freedom can work together towards shared goals, fostering a sense of unity and cooperation. Open communication about money and shared financial values can strengthen the bond between partners and build trust in the relationship. The ability to make sound financial decisions and plan for the future together can create a sense of security and stability in the relationship.

Financial freedom also enables individuals to support and uplift their loved ones. Whether it's providing for family members, contributing to shared expenses, or helping others in need, having financial stability can empower individuals to be more generous and supportive in their relationships. Moreover, financial independence can reduce the strain that financial issues can place on relationships, allowing partners to focus on building a strong emotional connection without the added stress of money worries.

By prioritizing financial education and empowering oneself with knowledge about money management, individuals can take control of their financial futures and ensure that their relationships are not hindered by financial struggles. By embracing a mindful approach to money and making conscious decisions about their finances, individuals can create a positive environment for their relationships to thrive. Financial freedom opens up possibilities for shared experiences, adventures, and dreams, strengthening the bond between partners and fostering a sense of unity and partnership in relationships.

Empowering Yourself through Financial Education

Financial education is a crucial tool in empowering individuals to take control of their financial well-being. By increasing your knowledge and understanding of financial concepts, you can make informed decisions about your money and secure your financial future.

Becoming financially literate involves learning about budgeting, saving, investing, managing debt, and planning for the long term. These foundational principles provide the framework for building a strong financial foundation.

Educating yourself about personal finance not only equips you with the skills to manage your money effectively but also empowers you to set and achieve financial goals. Whether you are looking to pay off debt, save for a major purchase, or invest for retirement, having a solid grasp of financial principles can guide you towards success.

There are numerous resources available to enhance your financial knowledge, including books, online courses, workshops, and financial advisors. Taking the time to educate yourself about money matters can lead to increased confidence in your financial decision-making and ultimately contribute to your overall financial well-being.

By committing to ongoing financial education, you are investing in yourself and your future. Embracing the opportunity to learn and grow in your financial knowledge will empower you to navigate the complexities of the financial world with confidence and clarity. Remember, financial education is not just a one-time endeavor but a lifelong journey towards building a secure and prosperous future.

Embracing Financial Independence as a Journey

Financial independence is not a destination to reach overnight; it is a journey that requires commitment, discipline, and perseverance. This journey is about taking control of your finances, setting goals, and actively working towards them. It involves making conscious choices about how you spend, save, and invest your money.

Embracing financial independence means understanding that it is a process that unfolds over time. It requires constant learning, adapting to changing financial circumstances, and staying focused on your long-term objectives. Challenges may arise along the way, but viewing them as opportunities for growth and learning can help you stay on track.

As you embark on this journey towards financial independence, remember that it is not just about accumulating wealth. It is also about finding peace of mind, security, and freedom from financial stress. By staying committed to your financial goals and making informed decisions, you are investing in your future and creating a life of abundance.

Financial independence is a worthwhile pursuit that can lead to a fulfilling and empowered life. Trust in your abilities, stay disciplined in your financial habits, and embrace the journey towards financial freedom with determination and optimism.

Conclusion: Living a Life of Financial Abundance

As you reflect on your journey towards financial independence, remember that living a life of financial abundance is not just about accumulating wealth, but about creating a sense of security and freedom in your life. By embracing the principles of financial literacy, mindful spending, and proactive planning, you have laid a strong foundation for your future financial success.

Financial abundance is not measured solely by the size of your bank account, but by the peace of mind and choices it affords you. It allows you to pursue your passions, support causes you believe in, and create lasting memories with loved ones. By making deliberate choices about how you earn, save, spend, and invest your money, you are empowering yourself to live a life aligned with your values and goals.

As you continue on your financial journey, remember that challenges may arise, but it is how you respond to them that defines your path towards abundance. Stay committed to your financial plan, adapt to changing circumstances, and seek support and guidance when needed. Celebrate your milestones along the way and use them as motivation to keep moving forward towards a future filled with financial abundance and security.

Your journey towards financial abundance is a testament to your commitment to creating a life of purpose, freedom, and fulfillment. By embodying the principles of financial independence and making conscious choices about your money, you are on a path towards a future where you can truly experience the joy and abundance that comes from being in control of your financial destiny.

Embracing Financial Independence

Introduction to Financial Independence

Financial independence is a concept that holds immense significance in today's world. It signifies the ability to sustain oneself financially without being reliant on external sources. Achieving financial independence is a goal that many aspire to attain, as it empowers individuals to have control over their financial destiny and live life on their own terms. It involves building a solid financial foundation that provides stability and security for the future.

Financial independence is not just about having a large bank account or material possessions; it is about having the freedom to make choices that align with your values and desires. It grants you the autonomy to pursue your passions, take calculated risks, and create a life that brings you fulfillment and happiness. It is a state of financial well-being that allows you to weather economic uncertainties and unexpected challenges with confidence and resilience.

Understanding the importance of financial independence is essential for setting meaningful financial goals and prioritizing your financial decisions. It serves as a guiding principle that shapes your mindset and approach towards money management. By striving towards financial independence, you are investing in your future self and laying the groundwork for a secure and prosperous life ahead.

Defining Financial Independence and Its Importance

Financial independence is a state of financial stability where you have enough income to cover your living expenses and achieve your financial goals without relying on external sources. It is about having control over your finances and the freedom to make choices that align with your values and aspirations. Financial independence provides a sense of security and peace of mind, knowing that you are not bound by financial constraints or obligations.

Achieving financial independence requires careful planning, discipline, and a long-term perspective. It involves assessing your current financial situation, setting clear goals, and taking deliberate steps to increase your income, reduce expenses, and build wealth. By prioritizing financial independence, you can create a path towards a more secure and fulfilling future for yourself and your loved ones.

The importance of financial independence cannot be overstated. It offers you the ability to pursue your passions, explore new opportunities, and take calculated risks without the fear of financial instability. It provides you with the freedom to make choices that align with your values and goals, rather than being driven by financial pressures or obligations. Financial independence is a key element of personal empowerment and self-reliance, allowing you to live life on your own terms and create a legacy that extends beyond financial wealth.

Steps to Achieving Financial Independence

Financial independence is a worthy goal that requires strategic planning and disciplined action. Achieving financial independence is not merely about accumulating wealth but also about creating a stable and sustainable financial future for yourself. To embark on the journey towards financial independence, you must start by assessing your current financial situation. This involves taking a detailed look at your income, expenses, assets, and liabilities. Understanding where you stand financially is crucial in setting realistic goals and formulating an effective plan to reach financial independence. By evaluating your financial health, you can identify areas that need improvement and make informed decisions about how to allocate your resources. Remember, achieving financial independence is a gradual process that requires patience, diligence, and perseverance. Start by tracking your expenses, creating a budget, and setting aside savings for emergencies and future investments. Establishing good financial habits, such as saving regularly, avoiding debt, and investing wisely, will set you on the right path towards financial independence. Additionally, consider increasing your income through side hustles, investment opportunities, or advancing in your career. Building multiple streams of income will not only boost your financial stability but also accelerate your journey towards financial independence. Keep in mind that financial independence is not a destination but a continuous pursuit of financial security and freedom. Stay focused on your goals, make informed financial decisions, and remain committed to your journey towards achieving true financial independence.

Assessing Your Current Financial Situation

Assessing Your Current Financial Situation

To truly understand where you stand on the path to financial independence, it is essential to assess your current financial situation with honesty and clarity. Begin by gathering all relevant financial documents, such as bank statements, credit card statements, investment accounts, and any other sources of income or expenses.

Next, create a detailed list of your assets and liabilities. Calculate your net worth by subtracting your total liabilities from your total assets. This will give you a clear picture of your current financial standing and help you identify areas for improvement.

Evaluate your income sources and expenses to determine your cash flow. Are you living within your means? Are there areas where you can cut back on expenses or increase your income? Understanding your cash flow is crucial in determining how much you can save and invest towards achieving financial independence.

Consider your debt levels and interest rates. Are you carrying high-interest debt that is holding you back from building wealth? Create a plan to pay off debt strategically and prioritize high-interest debt to free up more funds for savings and investments.

Lastly, analyze your savings and investment accounts. Are you saving enough for your future goals? Are your investments aligned with your risk tolerance and long-term objectives? Make adjustments as needed to ensure your financial resources are working towards your ultimate goal of financial independence.

By thoroughly assessing your current financial situation, you will be better equipped to make informed decisions and take the necessary steps towards achieving true financial independence and security.

Setting Clear Financial Goals and Objectives

Setting clear financial goals and objectives is a crucial step on the path to achieving true financial independence. Without a clear vision of what you want to accomplish, it can be challenging to stay motivated and focused on your journey. Begin by reflecting on your values, aspirations, and priorities. What truly matters to you in life? What do you want to achieve in the short and long term? Define your financial goals with clarity and specificity, making sure they are realistic and attainable. Break down your goals into measurable milestones and timelines to track your progress effectively. Whether you aim to become debt-free, purchase a home, save for retirement, or start a business, setting clear financial objectives will guide your actions and decisions towards a more secure and prosperous future. Make sure your goals are aligned with your unique circumstances and aspirations, allowing you to stay committed and motivated throughout your financial independence journey.

Creating a Detailed Financial Independence Plan

To create a detailed financial independence plan, you must first assess your current financial situation objectively. Look at your income, expenses, assets, and liabilities. Understand where you stand financially before you can plan where you want to be. Next, set specific and measurable financial goals that align with your vision of financial independence. Whether it's paying off debt, building savings, or investing for the future, your goals should be clear and achievable.

After setting your goals, devise a step-by-step plan to reach them. Break down your goals into smaller milestones and create a timeline for achieving each one. Consider the strategies and actions you need to take to move closer to financial independence. This may involve increasing your income through a side hustle or career advancement, cutting expenses to save more, or investing wisely to grow your wealth.

Don't forget to build an emergency fund to protect yourself from unexpected financial hardships. Having a safety net in place can prevent setbacks on your journey to financial independence. Additionally, review and adjust your plan regularly to reflect changes in your financial situation or goals. Flexibility and adaptability are key to staying on track and overcoming challenges along the way.

Remember, achieving financial independence is a marathon, not a sprint. Stay disciplined, stay focused, and stay committed to your plan. With determination and perseverance, you can pave the way to a future of financial stability and freedom.

Strategies for Increasing Income and Savings

Strategies for Increasing Income and Savings:

To secure your financial future and progress towards achieving true financial independence, it is crucial to adopt effective strategies that focus on both increasing your income and bolstering your savings. By implementing a combination of smart tactics and disciplined habits, you can pave the way towards a more secure and prosperous financial outlook.

One of the most fundamental steps in boosting your income is to actively seek opportunities for career advancement or additional sources of income. This may involve pursuing further education or training to enhance your skills and qualifications, positioning yourself for promotions or higher-paying job opportunities, or exploring side hustles and freelance opportunities to supplement your primary income stream.

In tandem with increasing your income, it is essential to prioritize saving and investing a portion of your earnings. Developing a habit of saving consistently, whether through automated transfers to a dedicated savings account or setting aside a percentage of your income each month, can build a strong foundation for financial stability. Additionally, creating a detailed budget that accounts for both necessities and discretionary spending can help you identify areas where you can cut back and redirect those funds towards savings.

Furthermore, consider exploring ways to maximize your savings through strategic financial planning. This could involve taking advantage of employer-sponsored retirement plans, such as 401(k) or IRA accounts, to benefit from tax advantages and potential employer matching contributions. Exploring investment opportunities, such as stocks, bonds, or real estate, can also provide avenues for growing your wealth over time.

Ultimately, the key to success in increasing income and savings lies in a combination of proactive measures, prudent financial decision-making, and a long-term perspective on building financial security. By consistently implementing these strategies and staying committed to your financial goals, you can set yourself on a path towards greater financial freedom and independence.

Building Passive Income Streams for Long-Term Stability

Passive income streams are a crucial aspect of financial independence, providing a stable source of income that requires minimal effort to maintain. One effective way to build passive income is through investments in dividend-paying stocks, bonds, or real estate. These assets can generate regular income without the need for active involvement, allowing you to steadily grow your wealth over time. Another popular method for creating passive income is through the creation of digital products such as e-books, online courses, or software applications. Once these products are developed and launched, they can continue to generate income with little ongoing effort on your part. Building a passive income portfolio requires careful planning and diversification to ensure long-term stability. By incorporating various income streams that suit your financial goals and risk tolerance, you can create a robust passive income foundation that will support you on your journey toward financial independence.

Overcoming Challenges and Roadblocks on the Path to Financial Independence

Financial independence is a lofty goal that many aspire to achieve, but the journey to get there is often fraught with challenges and roadblocks. One of the biggest obstacles on the path to financial independence is overcoming self-doubt and limiting beliefs. It's easy to feel overwhelmed by the enormity of the goal and to doubt whether you have what it takes to reach it. However, it's crucial to remember that financial independence is not an unattainable dream reserved for a select few – it is a realistic goal that anyone can work towards with dedication and perseverance.

Another common challenge on the road to financial independence is managing unexpected expenses and setbacks. Life is unpredictable, and while you may have a solid financial plan in place, unexpected expenses can quickly derail your progress. It's important to build a financial cushion to handle these unforeseen circumstances and to remain flexible in your approach to achieving financial independence.

Moreover, external factors such as economic downturns or job loss can also pose significant challenges on the path to financial independence. It's essential to have a contingency plan in place to weather these storms and to remain resilient in the face of adversity. Remember that setbacks are a natural part of the journey, and it's how you respond to these challenges that will ultimately determine your success.

Additionally, overcoming societal pressures and expectations can also be a hurdle on the path to financial independence. Society often promotes a culture of consumerism and instant gratification, making it difficult to stay focused on long-term financial goals. It's essential to tune out the noise and stay true to your values and priorities. By staying committed to your financial independence journey and making conscious choices that align with your goals, you can overcome these external pressures and stay on track towards achieving financial freedom.

In conclusion, while the road to financial independence may be filled with challenges and roadblocks, it is a journey that is worth embarking on. By overcoming self-doubt, managing unexpected expenses, navigating external factors, and resisting societal pressures, you can stay focused on your goal and achieve long-term financial success. Remember that financial independence is within your reach – all it takes is determination, resilience, and a steadfast commitment to your financial goals.

Embracing a Mindset of Financial Independence for Long-Term Success

To achieve long-term success in financial independence, it is crucial to cultivate a mindset that aligns with your goals and values. This mindset encompasses discipline, determination, and a strong belief in your ability to control your financial destiny. Embracing a mindset of financial independence requires a shift in perspective – viewing money not just as a means of survival, but as a tool for creating the life you desire.

One key aspect of this mindset is understanding that financial independence is a journey, not a destination. It requires consistent effort, dedication, and resilience to overcome challenges and setbacks along the way. By maintaining a long-term perspective and staying committed to your financial goals, you can build the foundation for lasting success.

Another important element of the financial independence mindset is the ability to delay gratification and make sacrifices in the present for a better future. This may involve cutting unnecessary expenses, increasing savings rates, or taking on additional income streams. By prioritizing your long-term financial well-being over short-term indulgences, you can set yourself up for greater freedom and security in the future.

Additionally, a mindset of financial independence involves taking responsibility for your financial decisions and outcomes. It means being proactive in managing your money, seeking out opportunities for growth and learning, and being willing to adapt to changing circumstances. By taking ownership of your financial future and staying proactive in your financial planning, you can pave the way for long-term success and stability.

Ultimately, embracing a mindset of financial independence is about believing in yourself and your ability to create the life you desire. It requires a commitment to personal growth, financial education, and continuous improvement. By adopting this mindset and staying focused on your goals, you can empower yourself to achieve lasting financial independence and build a secure future for yourself and your loved ones.

The Impact of Financial Literacy

Understanding the Foundation of Financial Literacy

Understanding the Foundation of Financial Literacy

Financial literacy is the cornerstone of personal and economic well-being. It is the knowledge and skills required to make informed decisions about money matters, manage financial resources effectively, and plan for the future. Without a solid understanding of financial concepts, individuals may find themselves struggling to navigate the complexities of the financial world.

At its core, financial literacy encompasses a range of topics, including budgeting, saving, investing, debt management, and retirement planning. These fundamental principles serve as the building blocks for financial success and stability. By equipping individuals with the necessary tools and knowledge, they can take control of their financial futures and achieve their goals.

Financial literacy empowers individuals to make sound financial decisions that align with their values and priorities. It provides them with the confidence to set financial goals, create a budget, and make informed choices about spending and saving. With a strong foundation in financial literacy, individuals are better equipped to weather financial challenges, avoid debt traps, and build wealth over time.

Moreover, financial literacy plays a crucial role in promoting economic development and reducing inequalities. When individuals are financially literate, they are more likely to participate in the economy, make wise investments, and contribute to overall financial stability. By spreading financial education and awareness, we can empower individuals from all walks of life to achieve financial independence and prosperity.

The Importance of Education on Money Matters

Financial literacy is more than just understanding the basics of money management—it is a critical skill that can empower individuals to take control of their financial future. In today's complex world, where financial decisions have far-reaching implications, the importance of education on money matters cannot be overstated.

Access to financial education equips individuals with the knowledge and tools needed to navigate the intricacies of personal finance. From budgeting and saving to investing and retirement planning, an understanding of money matters can lead to better financial outcomes and long-term stability.

Education on money matters also fosters a sense of empowerment and confidence in individuals to make informed decisions that align with their financial goals. By arming themselves with financial knowledge, individuals are better equipped to overcome financial challenges and seize opportunities for growth and prosperity.

Moreover, financial education serves as a powerful tool for breaking the cycle of financial illiteracy and promoting financial well-being across communities. By advocating for education on money matters, we can empower individuals to build a foundation of financial literacy that will support them throughout their lives.

In essence, the importance of education on money matters cannot be understated. It is a catalyst for empowerment, a shield against financial uncertainty, and a key ingredient in the recipe for financial success. By embracing the value of financial education, individuals can unlock a world of possibilities and take control of their financial destinies.

Empowering Individuals with Financial Knowledge

Empowering individuals with financial knowledge is a transformative journey that paves the way for a brighter financial future. It equips individuals with the necessary tools and understanding to make informed decisions, navigate financial challenges, and build a solid foundation for economic stability. Through education and awareness, individuals can break free from the shackles of financial uncertainty and take control of their financial well-being. Knowledge is power, and when it comes to finances, it holds the key to unlocking a world of opportunities and possibilities. By empowering individuals with financial knowledge, we empower them to create a life of security, abundance, and prosperity for themselves and their loved ones.

Breaking the Cycle of Financial Illiteracy

Breaking the Cycle of Financial Illiteracy

Financial illiteracy is a pervasive issue that affects individuals across all walks of life. From basic money management skills to complex investment strategies, the lack of financial knowledge can have far-reaching consequences. Breaking the cycle of financial illiteracy requires a concerted effort to educate and empower individuals to take control of their financial futures.

One of the first steps in combating financial illiteracy is to acknowledge the problem and its impact. Many individuals may not even realize they have gaps in their financial knowledge until they face a major financial decision or crisis. By raising awareness about the importance of financial literacy, we can begin to shift the mindset towards seeking out information and resources to improve financial understanding.

Education is key in breaking the cycle of financial illiteracy. Providing individuals with access to financial literacy programs, workshops, and resources can help bridge the knowledge gap and empower individuals to make informed decisions about their finances. From basic budgeting to understanding the nuances of investing, ongoing education can build a strong foundation for financial success.

It is also essential to address the underlying factors that contribute to financial illiteracy, such as lack of access to financial services, cultural taboos around money discussions, and systemic barriers to financial education. By identifying and dismantling these barriers, we can create a more inclusive and equitable financial landscape for all individuals.

Breaking the cycle of financial illiteracy requires a collaborative effort from individuals, communities, and policymakers. By working together to prioritize financial education and awareness, we can help individuals break free from the cycle of financial insecurity and pave the way for a brighter financial future.

Navigating the Complex World of Personal Finance

Navigating the complex world of personal finance requires a keen understanding of various financial concepts and tools. From budgeting to investing, individuals must equip themselves with the knowledge and skills necessary to make informed decisions about their money. Developing a solid financial plan tailored to one's goals and circumstances is crucial in achieving long-term financial stability. It involves setting realistic goals, monitoring expenses, building savings, and strategically managing debt. Moreover, staying informed about economic trends, investment opportunities, and regulatory changes can help individuals make prudent financial choices. Seeking advice from financial experts and leveraging technology for financial management can also streamline the process of navigating the intricacies of personal finance. In a world where financial decisions impact every aspect of our lives, mastering the art of personal finance is essential for building a secure financial future.

Making Informed Decisions for Long-Term Financial Stability

When it comes to achieving long-term financial stability, making informed decisions is paramount. Your financial choices today have a profound impact on your future financial well-being. It is crucial to consider factors such as your income, expenses, savings, investments, and debt management in order to set yourself up for a secure financial future.

Understanding the concept of budgeting is essential in managing your finances effectively. By creating a budget that aligns with your financial goals and lifestyle, you can track your spending, prioritize your expenses, and ensure that you are living within your means. This practice lays the foundation for financial stability and enables you to make informed decisions about where your money goes.

In addition to budgeting, it is important to consider the role of savings and investments in building long-term financial stability. Establishing an emergency fund can provide a safety net in times of financial uncertainty, while investing in assets that generate passive income can help you build wealth over time. By strategically allocating your money towards savings and investments, you can protect yourself against financial setbacks and work towards achieving your long-term financial goals.

Furthermore, when making financial decisions, it is crucial to conduct thorough research and seek advice from reputable sources. Whether you are considering a major purchase, planning for retirement, or managing your debt, seeking guidance from financial experts can help you make informed choices that align with your objectives. Educating yourself about various financial instruments and strategies can empower you to navigate the complex world of personal finance and make decisions that support your long-term financial stability.

Ultimately, making informed decisions for long-term financial stability requires a combination of discipline, knowledge, and planning. By taking a proactive approach to managing your finances and staying informed about economic trends and financial opportunities, you can position yourself for a secure and prosperous financial future.

Addressing Socioeconomic Disparities through Financial Literacy

Financial literacy plays a crucial role in addressing socioeconomic disparities. By providing individuals with the knowledge and skills to make informed financial decisions, we can help bridge the gap between different economic backgrounds. Understanding concepts such as budgeting, saving, investing, and debt management can empower individuals to take control of their financial futures, regardless of their socioeconomic status.

Access to financial education is key in leveling the playing field and breaking the cycle of poverty. By equipping individuals with the tools they need to navigate the complexities of personal finance, we can help them make progress towards achieving economic stability. This education can also lead to increased confidence in managing money, which can have a positive ripple effect on overall well-being and quality of life.

Furthermore, addressing socioeconomic disparities through financial literacy can help promote economic resilience in communities facing financial challenges. By empowering individuals with the knowledge to make sound financial choices, we can contribute to building stronger and more sustainable economies. This, in turn, can lead to greater opportunities for growth and prosperity for all members of society.

Overall, investing in financial literacy as a means to address socioeconomic disparities is not only a matter of economic importance but also a matter of social justice. By ensuring that everyone has access to the education and resources needed to achieve financial stability, we can work towards a more equitable and inclusive society.

Enhancing Economic Resilience through Education

Education serves as a powerful tool in enhancing economic resilience. By equipping individuals with the necessary financial knowledge and skills, education can help them navigate economic challenges and make informed decisions about their money. Financial education empowers individuals to set realistic financial goals, create and stick to budgets, manage debt effectively, and plan for the future. It also fosters a mindset of responsibility and discipline when it comes to money management, leading to greater financial stability and security. Through education, individuals can learn how to adapt to changing economic circumstances, build savings and investments, and ultimately enhance their overall economic resilience.

Transforming Mindsets and Behaviors towards Money

Transforming Mindsets and Behaviors towards Money

Financial literacy goes beyond just understanding numbers and concepts; it fundamentally involves transforming mindsets and behaviors towards money. Our relationship with money is deeply rooted in our beliefs, experiences, and attitudes, shaping how we earn, spend, save, and invest. To truly enhance our financial well-being, it is essential to shift our mindset towards a more empowered and intentional approach to managing our finances.

Breaking free from limiting beliefs and negative money narratives is the first step towards transforming our financial behaviors. Many of us have been conditioned to view money as a source of stress, scarcity, or conflict. By challenging these beliefs and reframing our perspective on money as a tool for growth, security, and freedom, we can begin to make more informed and empowered financial decisions.

Developing healthy financial habits is another essential aspect of transforming our behaviors towards money. This involves creating a budget, setting financial goals, tracking expenses, and consistently saving and investing for the future. By establishing a strong foundation of financial habits, we can build resilience against unexpected challenges and work towards achieving our long-term financial aspirations.

Cultivating a mindset of abundance and gratitude is also crucial in transforming our relationship with money. Instead of focusing on what we lack or comparing ourselves to others, practicing gratitude for what we have can shift our perspective towards abundance and contentment. This shift in mindset not only enhances our overall well-being but also influences our financial decisions from a place of positivity and empowerment.

Furthermore, fostering a growth mindset towards financial education and learning is key to continuous improvement and success. Recognizing that financial knowledge is a lifelong journey and being open to learning new strategies, tools, and concepts can expand our capabilities and enhance our financial literacy. By embracing a mindset of curiosity, growth, and adaptability, we can navigate the complexities of personal finance with confidence and resilience.

In essence, transforming mindsets and behaviors towards money is a transformative journey that requires self-awareness, intentionality, and commitment. By challenging limiting beliefs, developing healthy financial habits, cultivating gratitude and abundance, and embracing a growth mindset towards financial education, we can empower ourselves to create a more secure, fulfilling, and prosperous financial future.

Cultivating a Culture of Financial Literacy for Future Generations

As we strive to transform mindsets and behaviors towards money, it is crucial to consider the impact we can have on future generations. By cultivating a culture of financial literacy, we not only empower ourselves but also set the stage for a more financially knowledgeable and responsible society.

Our actions today will shape the financial landscape for our children and grandchildren. By instilling in them the values of saving, budgeting, investing, and financial independence, we equip them with the tools they need to navigate the complexities of money management.

Teaching financial literacy to the next generation is not just about practical skills but also about fostering a mindset of financial responsibility and independence. By starting these conversations early and leading by example, we can help our children develop healthy money habits that will serve them well throughout their lives.

One of the most powerful ways to cultivate a culture of financial literacy for future generations is through education. Schools play a crucial role in imparting financial knowledge to young minds, and it is essential to advocate for the inclusion of financial literacy in curricula at all levels.

Beyond the classroom, parents, guardians, and community leaders also have a significant role to play in shaping the financial habits of the younger generation. By engaging in open discussions about money, setting financial goals together, and encouraging smart financial decisions, we can plant the seeds for a financially literate future.

As we work towards cultivating a culture of financial literacy for future generations, let us remember the importance of leading by example and being proactive in our efforts to educate and empower the youth. Together, we can create a world where financial literacy is not just a skill but a way of life for generations to come.

Building Generational Wealth

Understanding the Importance of Long-Term Financial Planning

Long-term financial planning is a cornerstone of building generational wealth. It involves a careful and strategic approach to managing your finances with a focus on the future. By looking beyond immediate financial needs and considering the long-term impact of your decisions, you can set a strong foundation for financial stability and growth for yourself and future generations.

One key aspect of long-term financial planning is setting clear goals and objectives. This involves envisioning where you want to be financially in the next five, ten, or even twenty years, and then creating a roadmap to get there. By defining your financial goals, you can prioritize your efforts and make informed decisions that align with your long-term vision.

Another important aspect of long-term financial planning is mitigating risks and uncertainties. Economic conditions, market fluctuations, and unexpected events can all impact your financial well-being. By diversifying your investments, having a robust insurance coverage, and building an emergency fund, you can safeguard your finances against unforeseen circumstances and ensure long-term financial security.

Furthermore, long-term financial planning requires discipline and consistency. It's not just about making a single investment or setting a budget for a month - it's about consistently saving, investing, and monitoring your financial progress over the years. By staying committed to your financial plan and making adjustments as needed, you can stay on track towards achieving your long-term financial goals.

In essence, understanding the importance of long-term financial planning is essential for building generational wealth. By taking a proactive and strategic approach to managing your finances, you can lay the groundwork for a secure financial future for yourself and your heirs.

Passing Down Financial Values and Principles

Passing Down Financial Values and Principles

As we strive to build generational wealth, one of the most crucial aspects to consider is the passing down of financial values and principles. These values serve as the foundation upon which future generations can continue to grow and expand the family's wealth.

Parents and grandparents play a pivotal role in instilling these values early on in their children and grandchildren. By teaching the importance of saving, investing, and responsible spending, they set the stage for a lifetime of financial success. Values such as frugality, delayed gratification, and the significance of long-term planning are all key components that can be passed down through generations.

Furthermore, honesty, integrity, and ethical behavior in financial matters are essential principles to impart. Teaching the importance of transparency, accountability, and sound decision-making when it comes to money ensures that the family's wealth is not only preserved but also grown and protected for future generations.

It is also crucial to educate heirs on the value of wise financial management, including the risks and rewards of different investment strategies. By providing financial education and guidance, families empower their descendants to make informed decisions and navigate the complexities of the financial world with confidence and clarity.

Ultimately, passing down financial values and principles is a legacy that transcends monetary wealth. It is a gift that empowers future generations to build upon the foundation laid by their predecessors, ensuring the continued growth and prosperity of the family for years to come.

Investing in Education and Skill Development for Future Generations

Investing in education and skill development for future generations is a fundamental aspect of building generational wealth. Education is the key to unlocking opportunities and achieving financial success. By prioritizing education for your children and future generations, you are equipping them with the tools they need to thrive in a competitive world.

Education goes beyond the classroom - it instills values such as hard work, discipline, and critical thinking that are essential for financial prosperity. Encouraging a culture of continuous learning and self-improvement within your family ensures that future generations are well-prepared to navigate the ever-changing economic landscape.

Skill development is equally important in preparing the next generation for financial success. By identifying and nurturing individual talents and interests, you can help your children develop skills that will set them apart in their chosen fields. Whether it's through formal education, vocational training, or mentorship programs, investing in skill development enhances their employability and earning potential.

Moreover, fostering a mindset of entrepreneurship and innovation opens up new avenues for wealth creation. Encouraging creativity and risk-taking cultivates a spirit of resilience and adaptability, essential qualities for thriving in an increasingly competitive global economy.

By investing in education and skill development for future generations, you are not only securing their financial future but also laying the foundation for a legacy of success and prosperity that will endure for generations to come.

Leveraging Real Estate and Property Investments

Real estate and property investments offer a unique opportunity to build wealth and create a lasting legacy for future generations. By strategically leveraging real estate assets, individuals can not only generate passive income but also significantly increase their overall financial portfolio.

Investing in real estate provides a tangible and secure asset that has the potential for long-term appreciation. Whether through rental properties, commercial developments, or land investments, real estate offers a reliable way to grow wealth over time. By carefully selecting properties in high-demand areas and actively managing their investments, individuals can benefit from both rental income and property value appreciation.

Furthermore, real estate investments can serve as a hedge against inflation and economic fluctuations. Unlike stocks or other financial assets, real estate tends to retain its value and even increase in value during periods of economic growth. This stability can provide individuals with a sense of security and confidence in their overall financial strategy.

Additionally, real estate investments can provide tax advantages and deductions that can further enhance their financial benefits. Through strategies such as depreciation, mortgage interest deductions, and 1031 exchanges, investors can minimize their tax liabilities and maximize their returns on real estate investments.

In conclusion, leveraging real estate and property investments can play a crucial role in building generational wealth. By carefully selecting properties, actively managing investments, and leveraging tax advantages, individuals can create a robust financial portfolio that not only benefits themselves but also provides a solid foundation for future generations to thrive.

Establishing Trusts and Estate Planning Strategies

Establishing Trusts and Estate Planning Strategies

Estate planning is a critical component of building generational wealth. It involves more than just distributing assets after one's passing; it encompasses a comprehensive strategy to protect and preserve wealth for future generations. One powerful tool in estate planning is the establishment of trusts.

Trusts offer a structured way to transfer assets to beneficiaries while maintaining control over how those assets are managed and distributed. By setting up a trust, individuals can dictate specific conditions for asset distribution, such as age-based milestones or educational achievements. This ensures that wealth is passed down responsibly and in line with the values of the family.

Moreover, trusts can provide protection against creditors and lawsuits, safeguarding assets for future generations. They can also offer tax advantages, minimizing the tax burden on the estate and maximizing the amount of wealth that can be passed down to heirs.

When creating a trust, it is essential to work with experienced professionals, such as estate planners and attorneys, to ensure that the trust is structured in a way that aligns with your goals and objectives. By meticulously crafting a trust, individuals can create a lasting legacy that transcends generations, providing financial security and stability for their loved ones.

Incorporating trusts into your estate planning strategy is a proactive step towards safeguarding and growing your family's wealth. By carefully considering the structure and purpose of each trust, you can ensure that your assets are preserved and passed down in a manner that reflects your values and priorities. Trusts are a powerful tool that, when utilized effectively, can help secure the financial future of your family for years to come.

Navigating Tax Strategies for Wealth Preservation

Navigating Tax Strategies for Wealth Preservation

Tax planning is a crucial component of building and preserving generational wealth. Strategic tax management can help you minimize tax liabilities and maximize the growth of your assets over time. One key aspect of navigating tax strategies for wealth preservation is staying informed about tax laws and regulations that may impact your financial situation.

Working with a knowledgeable tax advisor or financial planner can help you identify opportunities for tax savings and implement effective strategies to optimize your tax position. Establishing a tax-efficient investment portfolio and considering tax-advantaged accounts can also play a significant role in preserving your wealth for future generations.

Furthermore, understanding the implications of inheritance taxes and estate taxes is essential in wealth preservation planning. Utilizing trusts, gifting strategies, and other estate planning tools can help reduce the tax burden on your heirs and ensure a smooth transfer of assets from one generation to the next.

When navigating tax strategies for wealth preservation, it is important to take a proactive approach and regularly review your financial plans to adapt to changes in tax laws and personal circumstances. By staying informed, seeking professional guidance, and making strategic decisions, you can protect and grow your wealth for the benefit of future generations.

Creating Multiple Streams of Passive Income

It's essential for individuals seeking to build generational wealth to diversify their income streams to ensure long-term financial stability. Creating multiple sources of passive income can significantly contribute to this goal. Passive income refers to earnings received with little to no ongoing effort required from the recipient. This type of income can come from various sources, such as investments, royalties, rental income, and affiliate marketing.

Investing in dividend-paying stocks can be a reliable way to generate passive income. By owning shares in successful companies that regularly distribute dividends to their shareholders, individuals can earn a steady stream of income without actively managing the investments. Dividend income can serve as a consistent source of cash flow that can be reinvested to further grow the investment portfolio.

Another avenue for passive income is through rental properties. Investing in real estate and renting out properties can provide a continuous source of income through rental payments. However, it's important to conduct thorough research and due diligence before diving into real estate investing to ensure the properties are profitable and well-maintained.

Creating digital products or online courses can also be a lucrative source of passive income. By leveraging one's expertise and skills to develop informational products that can be sold online, individuals can generate income on an ongoing basis. This approach requires an upfront investment of time and effort to create the product but can yield passive income for years to come.

Additionally, affiliate marketing involves promoting products or services and earning a commission for each sale made through the affiliate link. By partnering with reputable companies and promoting their products to a targeted audience, individuals can earn passive income through affiliate marketing efforts.

Diversifying passive income streams can provide financial security and stability for individuals and their future generations. By strategically investing in various income-generating opportunities, individuals can build a resilient financial foundation that withstands economic fluctuations and contributes to long-term wealth preservation.

Fostering Entrepreneurship and Business Succession Planning

Fostering Entrepreneurship and Business Succession Planning

As you build your family's wealth, it is essential to consider the role of entrepreneurship and business succession planning. Encouraging entrepreneurial endeavors within your family can create opportunities for growth and financial independence. By instilling an entrepreneurial mindset in future generations, you pave the way for innovation and sustainable wealth creation.

Successful business succession planning ensures the seamless transfer of assets and responsibilities from one generation to the next. Establishing a clear succession plan early on can help mitigate conflicts and ensure the continuity of your family's business legacy. It is crucial to identify and groom potential successors, provide them with the necessary skills and experience, and involve them in key decision-making processes.

Effective communication and collaboration among family members are integral to successful entrepreneurship and business succession planning. Open dialogue about goals, expectations, and roles within the business can foster unity and alignment among family members. By creating a shared vision for the future of the business, you can strengthen familial bonds and work towards common objectives.

Moreover, seeking professional guidance from advisors and mentors can provide valuable insights and expertise in navigating the complexities of entrepreneurship and succession planning. Legal and financial advisors can help you develop strategies to protect your business assets, minimize tax implications, and ensure a smooth transition of ownership.

By fostering entrepreneurship and implementing a robust business succession plan, you lay the groundwork for long-term financial stability and sustainability for future generations. Embracing innovation, collaboration, and strategic planning can empower your family to thrive as business owners and custodians of generational wealth.

Promoting Philanthropy and Giving Back to the Community

Promoting philanthropy and giving back to the community is a noble and essential practice that goes beyond financial wealth. It is a way to contribute positively to society, create a lasting impact, and instill values of generosity and compassion in future generations.

Engaging in philanthropy allows families to support causes they are passionate about, whether it be in education, healthcare, environmental conservation, or social justice. By giving back to the community, families can address social issues, make a difference in the lives of others, and leave a positive legacy for generations to come.

Through thoughtful planning and strategic giving, families can maximize the impact of their philanthropic efforts. Establishing a clear mission and vision for philanthropy, setting measurable goals, and involving family members in decision-making processes can ensure that resources are allocated effectively and that the causes supported align with the family's values and priorities.

Furthermore, promoting philanthropy within the family can strengthen bonds, foster a sense of unity, and instill a sense of responsibility and purpose in future generations. By involving children and grandchildren in philanthropic activities, such as volunteering, fundraising, or serving on nonprofit boards, families can pass down values of empathy, altruism, and social responsibility.

In addition to individual giving, families can also explore avenues for collective impact through family foundations, donor-advised funds, or strategic partnerships with nonprofit organizations. By pooling resources and expertise, families can amplify their philanthropic efforts, leverage their impact, and create sustainable change in their communities.

Ultimately, promoting philanthropy and giving back to the community is not just about making financial contributions; it is about making a difference, fostering connections, and leaving a meaningful legacy that extends far beyond financial wealth. By embracing the spirit of philanthropy, families can create a lasting impact that shapes the future for generations to come.

Sustaining Family Unity and Financial Harmony across Generations

Ensuring that financial harmony endures through the generations requires deliberate effort and a shared commitment to family unity. Communication is key in fostering understanding and respect among family members when it comes to financial matters. Open and honest discussions about financial values, goals, and responsibilities can help build a strong foundation for collaboration and collaboration across generations.

Establishing clear guidelines and expectations for financial decision-making and wealth management can help prevent misunderstandings and conflicts. Creating a family constitution or wealth management plan that outlines roles, responsibilities, and processes for decision-making can provide clarity and structure for future generations.

Encouraging financial education and literacy within the family can empower individuals to make informed decisions and take ownership of their financial future. Providing opportunities for learning about investments, budgeting, and wealth preservation can help equip family members with the knowledge and skills they need to navigate the complexities of managing inherited wealth.

Fostering a culture of shared values and shared goals can help unify family members and strengthen their bond. By promoting values such as integrity, generosity, and social responsibility, families can establish a common purpose that transcends individual interests and fosters a sense of unity and solidarity.

Seeking professional guidance and advice from financial planners, estate planners, and wealth managers can provide valuable insights and strategies for preserving wealth and ensuring its smooth transfer to future generations. By leveraging the expertise of professionals, families can create robust structures and mechanisms for safeguarding their financial legacy and promoting financial harmony across generations.

Ultimately, sustaining family unity and financial harmony requires a collective commitment to communication, education, values, and professional guidance. By working together and upholding shared principles and goals, families can build a lasting legacy of financial stability, unity, and prosperity for generations to come.

Mastering the Art of Financial Resilience

Understanding the Concept of Financial Resilience

Financial resilience is the ability to adapt and bounce back from financial challenges and setbacks. It involves staying strong and determined in the face of adversity, maintaining a positive outlook, and actively seeking solutions to overcome obstacles. Developing financial resilience is essential for navigating the ups and downs of the ever-changing financial landscape. It requires a mindset of perseverance, resourcefulness, and flexibility to withstand financial pressures and uncertainties. By understanding the concept of financial resilience, individuals can cultivate the strength and resilience needed to thrive in challenging financial circumstances.

Developing a Resilient Mindset

Developing a resilient mindset is crucial in facing the challenges that may arise in your financial journey. It involves cultivating a steadfast determination and a positive outlook towards setbacks and obstacles. Resilience allows you to bounce back from financial difficulties, learn from your mistakes, and continue to move forward with confidence.

To develop a resilient mindset, you must be willing to embrace challenges and view them as opportunities for growth. By facing your financial fears head-on and staying committed to your long-term goals, you can build mental toughness and perseverance.

In times of financial stress, it is essential to remain calm and rational, focusing on solutions rather than dwelling on problems. By maintaining a clear and focused mindset, you can navigate through uncertainties and make sound financial decisions.

Building resilience also involves accepting that setbacks are a natural part of any financial journey. Instead of being discouraged by failures, use them as learning experiences to strengthen your resolve and determination.

Moreover, surrounding yourself with a supportive network of family, friends, and financial advisors can provide you with the guidance and encouragement needed to stay resilient in the face of challenges. Seeking advice from those who have faced similar situations can offer valuable perspectives and insights.

Ultimately, developing a resilient mindset requires a combination of self-awareness, determination, and adaptability. By cultivating these qualities, you can weather any financial storm and emerge stronger and more resilient than ever before.

Building Emergency Funds and Contingency Plans

Building Emergency Funds and Contingency Plans

Establishing a financial safety net is crucial in safeguarding yourself against unforeseen circumstances. Start by setting aside a portion of your income each month into an emergency fund. This fund should ideally cover at least three to six months' worth of living expenses.

Create a budget that prioritizes saving for emergencies and allocate a specific amount towards this fund regularly. Consider automating your savings to ensure consistency and discipline in building your emergency fund.

In addition to saving, it's essential to have a contingency plan in place for different scenarios such as job loss, medical emergencies, or unexpected home repairs. Identify potential risks and outline steps to mitigate their impact on your finances.

Review your insurance coverage to ensure you are adequately protected in case of emergencies. This includes health insurance, disability insurance, homeowners or renters insurance, and life insurance, depending on your individual circumstances.

Stay proactive by regularly reassessing your emergency fund and contingency plans to adjust for any changes in your financial situation or lifestyle. Being prepared for unforeseen events will provide you with peace of mind and financial security in challenging times.

Adapting to Financial Crises and Uncertainties

During times of financial crises and uncertainties, it is imperative to remain calm and composed. The ability to adapt to challenging situations is a crucial skill that can make a significant difference in your financial well-being. When faced with unexpected setbacks such as job loss, medical emergencies, or economic downturns, it is essential to evaluate your financial situation realistically and take swift action to mitigate the impact.

One of the first steps in adapting to financial crises is to assess your current financial standing. Take stock of your assets, debts, and expenses to understand the extent of the challenge you are facing. Create a detailed budget that prioritizes essential expenses and identifies areas where you can cut back or reduce spending. By gaining a clear picture of your financial situation, you can make informed decisions about how to weather the storm.

In times of crisis, it may be necessary to explore alternative sources of income or financial assistance. Consider picking up temporary or freelance work, selling unused items, or seeking government aid programs that can provide temporary relief. Additionally, reaching out to friends, family, or community resources for support can alleviate some of the financial pressures you may be facing.

Maintaining open communication with creditors and financial institutions is key during times of uncertainty. If you are struggling to make payments on loans, mortgages, or credit cards, proactively contact your lenders to discuss potential options for deferment, forbearance, or restructuring. By being transparent about your situation and seeking assistance when needed, you can avoid further financial strain and protect your credit score.

It is also crucial to prioritize your mental and emotional well-being during financial crises. Practice self-care, seek support from loved ones, and consider speaking to a financial advisor or counselor for guidance. Remember that financial challenges are temporary, and with resilience, determination, and a strategic approach, you can navigate through uncertainties and emerge stronger on the other side.

Leveraging Resources and Support Networks

During times of financial crisis or uncertainty, it is crucial to leverage the resources and support networks available to you. Building a strong support system can provide you with guidance, advice, and emotional reassurance during challenging times.

Reach out to trusted friends, family members, or financial advisors who can offer valuable insights and perspective on your situation. Surround yourself with individuals who have a positive influence on your financial well-being and can help you navigate through tough decisions.

Networking within professional circles or financial communities can also be beneficial in expanding your knowledge and resources. Joining financial forums, attending workshops, or seeking mentorship from experienced individuals can provide you with valuable information and strategies for overcoming financial hurdles.

Utilize online resources and tools to access a wealth of information on financial planning, budgeting, and investment strategies. Websites, apps, and online communities offer a plethora of resources to help you make informed decisions and stay on track with your financial goals.

Consider seeking the expertise of a financial planner or counselor who can provide personalized advice and strategies tailored to your specific financial situation. These professionals can offer a holistic view of your finances and help you create a roadmap for achieving financial stability and resilience.

Remember that you are not alone in facing financial challenges, and reaching out for support is a sign of strength, not weakness. By leveraging your resources and support networks, you can build a solid foundation for financial resilience and set yourself up for long-term success.

Resilient Financial Planning and Decision-Making

Resilient Financial Planning and Decision-Making:

Navigating the complexities of financial planning and decision-making requires a steadfast commitment to resilience. It is during times of uncertainty and challenge that the true test of our financial acumen emerges. To cultivate resilience in our financial endeavors, it is essential to approach planning and decision-making with a blend of prudence, foresight, and adaptability.

In the realm of financial planning, having a clear understanding of one's financial goals and priorities is paramount. Setting realistic and achievable objectives provides a solid foundation for making informed decisions. By aligning our monetary strategies with our long-term aspirations, we can steer our financial ship towards success even in turbulent waters.

Decisiveness is a key trait when it comes to making financial decisions. The ability to weigh the pros and cons of various options, assess risks, and follow through with calculated choices can make a significant difference in our financial journey. In times of uncertainty, having a well-thought-out plan and the confidence to execute it can mitigate potential setbacks and propel us closer to our goals.

Risk management plays a crucial role in resilient financial planning. Diversifying investments, establishing emergency funds, and staying informed about economic trends are integral components of a robust financial strategy. By proactively safeguarding our financial interests and preparing for contingencies, we can build a resilient financial framework capable of withstanding unforeseen challenges.

Furthermore, staying abreast of market developments and seeking advice from financial experts can offer valuable insights for making sound financial decisions. Leveraging the expertise of professionals and utilizing cutting-edge tools can enhance our financial decision-making capabilities and optimize our financial outcomes.

In essence, resilient financial planning and decision-making require a harmonious blend of strategy, fortitude, and adaptability. By proactively planning for the future, exercising prudence in decision-making, and learning from past experiences, we can navigate the complexities of the financial landscape with resilience and confidence.

Learning from Past Mistakes and Failures

Mistakes and failures are a natural part of our financial journey. They provide valuable lessons that shape our financial decisions and attitudes. Reflecting on past missteps allows us to learn, grow, and become more resilient in our financial planning. When we acknowledge our mistakes, we can transform them into stepping stones towards a more secure financial future.

It's essential to examine the reasons behind our failures and take responsibility for our actions. Whether it's overspending, making risky investments, or neglecting savings, understanding the root causes of our financial setbacks is the first step towards improvement. By identifying patterns and triggers that lead to mistakes, we can develop strategies to avoid repeating them in the future.

Learning from past mistakes also involves adjusting our mindset and behavior. Accepting failure as a learning opportunity rather than a defeat empowers us to approach financial challenges with resilience and determination. By reframing our setbacks as temporary setbacks rather than insurmountable obstacles, we open ourselves up to new possibilities and growth.

Moreover, seeking guidance from financial experts, mentors, or trusted advisors can provide valuable insights and perspectives on our past mistakes. Their experience and expertise can offer fresh perspectives and strategies for overcoming financial challenges. Listening to their advice and incorporating their recommendations into our financial planning can help us avoid repeating past errors.

In conclusion, the key to learning from past mistakes and failures is humility, self-reflection, and a willingness to change. By embracing our flaws and shortcomings, we can turn them into strengths that propel us towards a more resilient and successful financial future.

Resilience in Investments and Wealth Management

Embarking on the journey of financial resilience requires a strategic approach towards investments and wealth management. As you navigate the volatile terrain of financial markets, it is essential to cultivate a resilient mindset that can withstand fluctuations and uncertainties. Diversification is key in spreading risk and ensuring a stable foundation for your financial portfolio. Allocate your assets across various investment vehicles to minimize potential losses and maximize opportunities for growth.

Stay informed and vigilant about market trends and economic indicators that may impact your investments. Conduct thorough research and seek advice from financial experts to make informed decisions about where to allocate your funds. Remember that long-term success in wealth management requires patience and discipline. Avoid impulsive decisions driven by emotions, and instead, stick to your predetermined investment strategy.

In times of economic downturn or market volatility, resist the urge to panic-sell your investments. Stay focused on your long-term financial goals and trust in the resilience of your diversified portfolio. Consider seeking opportunities to buy low and sell high when market conditions present themselves. Remember that resilience in investments is not about avoiding risks altogether, but rather managing risks effectively to weather the storms and emerge stronger on the other side.

Monitor your investments regularly and make adjustments as needed to adapt to changing market conditions. Stay proactive in reviewing your investment strategy and consider rebalancing your portfolio to maintain alignment with your financial objectives. Keep a vigilant eye on fees and expenses associated with your investments, as minimizing costs can have a significant impact on your overall returns.

Embrace the principles of financial resilience in your wealth management approach, cultivating a strategic mindset that prioritizes long-term sustainability over short-term gains. By diversifying your investments, staying informed, and maintaining discipline in your strategy, you can build a robust financial foundation that withstands the test of time. Trust in your resilience and commitment to wealth management as you navigate the complexities of the financial landscape.

Staying Committed to Financial Resilience

Committing to financial resilience requires unwavering dedication and discipline. It is not enough to simply understand the concepts and strategies; one must actively practice them in daily life. Building resilience in your financial habits takes consistent effort and a mindset focused on long-term stability.

Staying committed means making deliberate choices that align with your financial goals, even when faced with temptations or obstacles. It involves setting clear boundaries for your spending, saving diligently, and continuously reevaluating your financial decisions to ensure they support your overall resilience.

Creating a routine that reinforces your commitment to financial resilience can be incredibly beneficial. Whether it's setting aside a specific time each week to review your financial progress, tracking your expenses diligently, or regularly updating your budget to reflect changing circumstances, establishing these habits can help you stay on track even during challenging times.

Resilience is not just about weathering storms; it's also about bouncing back stronger and more prepared for future challenges. By staying committed to your financial resilience journey, you are investing in your future self and building a solid foundation for long-term financial success. Celebrate each small victory along the way, and use them as motivation to continue your journey towards financial stability and security.

Celebrating Resilience and Achievements

As you reflect on your journey towards financial resilience, take a moment to acknowledge and celebrate the progress you have made. Each step taken, each obstacle overcome, and each lesson learned has contributed to your growth and strength in managing your finances. It is important to recognize and appreciate the effort and dedication you have put into building a solid foundation for your financial well-being.

Celebrate your resilience by setting aside time to reflect on your achievements, both big and small. Whether it's reaching a savings goal, successfully navigating a financial challenge, or making a wise investment decision, each milestone is a testament to your perseverance and determination. Share your successes with your loved ones, celebrate with a special meal or treat yourself to something that brings you joy.

Remember to express gratitude for the support and guidance you have received along the way. Be thankful for the resources and tools that have helped you stay on track, and for the people who have believed in you and encouraged you to keep going. Recognize that financial resilience is not built in isolation, but through a collective effort of learning, growing, and adapting to life's financial ups and downs.

As you celebrate your resilience and achievements, take a moment to also reflect on the challenges you have faced and the lessons you have learned. Use these experiences as stepping stones towards continued growth and improvement in your financial journey. Stay committed to your goals, maintain a positive mindset, and continue to build on your financial resilience for a brighter and more secure future.

www.ingramcontent.com/pod-product-compliance
Lightning Source LLC
Chambersburg PA
CBHW052256220526
45471CB00001B/361